THE GOOD RAIN

VOLUME II

The Sisters of
St. Joseph of Rochester
in Brazil
2001-2024

THE GOOD RAIN
Volume II

The Sisters of
St. Joseph of Rochester
in Brazil
2001-2024

by Monica Weis SSJ

Printed in the United States of America

The Good Rain, Volume II: The Sisters of St. Joseph of Rochester
in Brazil 2001-2024/ 1st Edition

ISBN: 978-1-953610-73-7

Nonfiction> Social Responsibility
Nonfiction> Religious Orders>Catholic
Nonfiction> International>Brazil
Nonfiction> Biography, Memoir

Cover design: Mary Anne Turner SSJ

Photographs: Archives, Sisters of St. Joseph of Rochester

Cover photo: Rio Paranaiba before the town of Paranaiguara was flooded, 1977

NFB Publishing
119 Dorchester Road
Buffalo, New York 14213
For more information visit Nfbpublishing.com

For the 37 Sisters of St. Joseph of Rochester
who have lived and served in Brazil,
especially Sisters Katherine and Suzanne
who are lovingly buried in *Jardim do Cerrado*.

ACKNOWLEDGEMENTS

MORE THAN A perfunctory list of thanks, this page acknowledges the commitment of our Sisters in Brazil, their deep wisdom and their ongoing assistance with this project. Of particular note is Sister Maureen Finn, whose memory for dates and facts is astounding, and Sister Jean Bellini, whose eagle eye noted not only missing Portuguese accents, but also scrutinized the contextual accuracy and interpretation of events. A sincere word of appreciation goes to Sister Ellen Kuhl who, more than a year ago suggested I might be interested in chronicling these last twenty years of our mission in Brazil, and who nudged me toward our SSJ Archives and auxiliary sources of information. The SSJ Archives, of course, is the special domain of Kathy Urbanic, archivist *extrordinaire* whose quick response and patience with my initial fumbling helped immerse me in folders and folders of documents, reports, letters, and clippings. For Sister Anne Marvin's gift of storytelling and humor, I am ever grateful. Many of the recounted vignettes in this book were offered with a chuckle by Anne and supplemented the data I was mining from the Annual Reports. Unless otherwise stated, the facts and events recounted in these pages were retrieved from archival documents, Zoom meetings and in-person conversations with our sisters. A special word of thanks to Sister Anita Kurowski and Martha Mortensen-Kolkmann for their willingness to recount the experience of their brief time in Brazil, identify the activities they participated in, and share the life lessons of living in a Brazilian culture. Lastly, I am grateful to the previous SSJ Rochester Leadership team (Sisters Eileen Daly, Beth Sutter, Elaine Englert, and Marilyn Pray) for their affirmation of this writing project, as well as the current team (Sisters Mary Lou Mitchell, Beth Sutter, Anita Kurowski, Elaine Hollis) for their support in bringing this project to publication during the 60th year of celebration of our mission in Brazil. To all my friends and sisters: *Obrigada*.

Table of Contents

THE GOOD RAIN - VOLUME II

*"In the first book, Theophilus, I wrote about all that Jesus did
and taught from the beginning..." (Acts 1:1)*

PROLOGUE

IN THE FIRST book, dear reader, our beloved Sister Margaret Brennan wrote about the *first* forty years of the Sisters of St. Joseph of Rochester's mission in Brazil: the great sendoff of five Sisters to Mateira, the early days of teaching and administering the *ginasio*, the expansion of ministry into pastoral presence in the various church communities, involvement in health care (Paranaiguara, Itaguaçu), civic and health councils, community organizing for land reform, diocesan vocation ministry, outreach to our indigenous brothers and sisters, and the joyous celebration of the first profession of Sister Maria José.

This account will focus on the sisters' growing sensitivity to the realities of life in Brazil, the increasing violence in both cities and rural areas, the need to respond to nearby and not-so-nearby disasters such as in Peru, and the challenges of reaching out to new ministries in new geographic areas, and the creation of a cadre of Associates. In each instance, the sisters were conscious of the importance of their presence among the people and the need to support local efforts for social justice. And there were times of celebration, too: Sister Ireny's and Sister Joana's 25th anniversary of profession, and later Sister Maria José's final profession, the 40th and 50th anniversary of the Sisters of St. Joseph of Rochester in Brazil, and the challenges of a new intercongregational ministry and creating a new or central house. This volume will trace the evolution of their mission in Brazil, its highpoints and low points, and the ongoing priority of responding to the needs of the times.

CHAPTER 1

Tendrils of New Growth 2001-2004

THE EARLY YEARS of the twenty-first century were a flurry of activity in each of the SSJ locations. Sister Maria José Monteiro de Oliveira renewed her vows and began studies in law school; Sister Elizabete Alves Gama (Bete) professed her first vows and began preparation for college with a plan to earn a psychology degree; both Elizabete and Maria José attended an inter-congregational program for Sisters in Temporary Vows offered by the Brazilian Conference of Religious; Sister Jean Bellini, already working for the Pastoral Land Commission began a new training program at the national level, focusing on the anthropology, cultural identity of rural workers, history and current social movements in rural areas. And in the various communities, the sisters continued forming the laity for ministry by training volunteers for baptism/ confirmation preparation, expanding the team of catechists, coordinating biblical reflection groups, celebrating Liturgy of the Word, and coaching adults for home visitations. Although few in number, the sisters were reaching people, being pastoral agents, accompanying small communities, and contributing to civil policy in three different states: Goiás, Mato Grosso, and Minas Gerais.[1] Each location had its pluses and minuses.

The larger world also had its pluses and minuses. In those early years of the twenty-first century, Wikipedia, Facebook, and YouTube were launched; George W. Bush was inaugurated as the 43rd President of the United States; Silvio Berlusconi was elected Prime Minister of Italy; and Queen Elizabeth II celebrated her Golden Jubilee. Steve Fossett was the first person to fly solo non-stop abound the world; and the Euro became the currency of exchange in Western Europe. Yet there were also minuses in the form of disasters: devastating earthquakes in India, Kashmir, Pakistan and Afghanistan; the explosion of the shuttle Challenger killing all seven astronauts; eleven members of the royal family in Nepal murdered by the Prince who then took his own life; and the catastrophic disaster of September 11—the four hijacked planes that destroyed the Twin Towers in New York City, parts of the Pentagon in Washington, and the crash in Stonycreek Township, Pennsylvania, a tragedy costing nearly 3000 lives. The world watched in horror as the scene was replayed around the globe on TV, computers, and phones.

Sister Joana recalls that she was in Rio taking an academic course. She immediately thought of the sisters in Goiânia and Rochester. Sister Anne remembers that she was home alone in Uberlândia when a neighbor came to the house shouting, "Turn on your TV!" Sister Jean was not in Brazil but at her father's house on Long Island, NY. Sister Maureen was accompanying an outlying parish celebrating the Feast of Our Lady of Mercy when a woman told her she heard about the attack on her battery-operated radio. Her son, coming into the house said "What's the problem? Oh, that has nothing to do with us." The mother immediately scolded him: "Those are our brothers and sisters." In the following days the sisters felt much support from the people. They were "so sad for us." Yet once the United States retaliated by invading Iraq and vowing vengeance on the perpetrators, "their sympathy declined." One young man at a parish festival lit into Maureen: "The US got what it deserved." How could such a superpower flaunt its power? How could the leader of the free world exhibit such vengeance? The sisters, too, "were proud of being a Sister of St. Joseph of Rochester, yet felt a sense of shame for belonging to a country that is always attacking."[2] Both feelings were in conflict. Those were days of tension and disillusionment, yet the mission of the sisters continued.

GoIÁS

In Goiânia Sisters Anne Marvin, Janet Connorton, Katherine Popowich, Ellen Kuhl, Suzanne Wills, and Elizabete Alves Gama were pastoral agents accompanying the people in five communities covering seven regions of the city. The diocesan theme in 2001 was "Popular Missions"—an initiative to motivate members to be missionaries by visiting their neighbors, praying with families, and being alert to potential problems. Once a team of volunteers was trained, the "missionaries" were well received because of their ecumenical attitude which, in turn, resulted in greater participation among the members of the community. Many of the sisters began serving on local Councils. These gatherings were a bit different from our American concept of a council. Frequently, Brazilian governing bodies rely on Civilian Councils for ideas and clout. Their main focus is civil advocacy for social problems such as health, education, public safety, or the environment. Their primary value is being watchdogs on the use of money supplied by the government. Although Citizen Councils were established by the new 1988 Federal Constitution, they were sometimes resisted by the authorities.

The region in Goiânia where the sisters lived had neither a hospital nor paved streets, and so was named by the people "*Alto da Poeira*" (the Dusty Heights). The area was just beginning to organize health clinics, so Sister Katherine was quick to lend her presence to the effort. Sister Anne remembers that Katherine was instrumental in reminding the municipal government about the large number of families living in *Alto da Poeira* and that they needed a hospital of their own. Indeed, since 1998 Sister Katherine had been active on three health councils: local, municipal and regional. She became a member of the Municipal Health Council in Goiânia, representing a local organization, and subsequently was elected President of it in 2000.[3]

Katherine believed in the power of "the manner in which we do what we do." By creating relationships, she helped improve the whole health care system. For example, Katherine invited the government level health secretary to dinner. Breaking bread together in a more casual setting enabled her to press for better health care structures so that eventually all seven districts in Goiânia had monthly meetings for a health forum. Not long after, a mental health facility was built, an urgent care resource was available, and improved clinics became training sites for medical students. None of this happened overnight, but Katherine's presence in the health councils encouraged the other members to persist in making their needs known. In response, the government leaders moved forward with courage and understanding. During the days when the government provided Katherine with a car and driver to enable her to visit various sites, she would always engage the driver in conversation, even bringing him bread or a cake. Katherine knew that it was all about building relationships— "the manner in which we do what we do."

Through Katherine's persistent efforts, a public Maternity Hospital now operates twenty-four hours a day in the northwest region of Goiânia and focuses on humanizing the birthing process. Memory has it that Katherine was behind this success. She was approached by an obstetrician interested in practicing in a hospital emphasizing natural childbirth. According to Sister Anne Marvin, "The doctor and the nun got the families, especially the women, behind them, and the result was that the government had no choice but to build a prize-winning hospital with all the specifications necessary for humanized natural childbirth."[4] Not surprisingly, the Hospital, committed to practicing natural childbirth, became a model of care for the surrounding area. In Katherine's honor, *Maternidade Nascer Cidadão* now carries a double name: the Portuguese phrase "born as a citizen" followed by the name of Irmã Katherine Popowich.'

Sister Katherine also encouraged Sister Anne Marvin to run for the Local Health Council of the Maternity Hospital. After the votes were counted, however, Anne came in third on the waiting list, but by the time of the group's second monthly meeting, the other candidates had dropped out, so Anne became a counselor. Eventually she became the Coordinator of the Council. Comprised of one half hospital administrators and employees and one half local citizens, the Council operated with 15-20 members.

In addition to her work as Coordinator, Anne discovered she could travel around the neighborhoods and meet with her base communities more efficiently on her new motorbike.[5]

In Parque Tremendão, Sister Joana Mendes was preparing for the Martyrs' Pilgrimage and the National Conference of Religious Formation, while Sister Ellen Kuhl was coordinating ten groups of the Pastoral of the Child, teaching young mothers the value of good nutrition and encouraging them to help their children thrive better by giving them massage therapy. As one of the initiatives of the National Council of Brazilian Bishops, the Pastoral of the Child is an organized effort to support mothers of children under six. Founded by Dr. Zilda Arns Neumann, a progressive Brazilian laywoman and sister of Cardinal Paulo Evaristo Arns, the initiative began in 1983 to combat high infant mortality rate through government funding and a campaign by the major TV networks. In one year of activities, they were successful in reducing the infant mortality rate from 127 per thousand born to 28 per thousand born.[6] Trained teams of volunteers made home visits, sponsored monthly meetings about low-cost nutrition and home remedies, and weighed children to track their growth and flourishing. The program was so successful that after a number of years, the practice was incorporated into the routine of the local units of the national Family Health Care Program. In the years since then, the pastoral has shrunk in size, and the Church adjusted its focus to the elderly, whose numbers were growing.[7]

ITAGUAÇU

Sister Barbara Orczyk continued as administrator of her parish in Itaguaçu (since Fr. Jeremiah Donovan OMI resided in Paranaiguara) and even though she was not a Brazilian citizen, Barbara was elected to represent the District of Itaguaçu on the Municipal Public Safety Council of São Simão (December 2000), and supervised the renovation of the health care center in Itaguaçu. In March 2004, she was honored by the Municipal legislature at the International Day of Women.[8]

In Paranaiguara, Sr. Christel Burgmaier, a credentialed nurse, continued her work in the Municipal Hospital where she coordinated the nursing staff, oversaw pre-natal care, surgery, x-ray, and, as part of the Family Health Care Program (PSF), supervised fifteen in-service student nurses, and presented programs for pregnant women. In her parish, Chris both coordinated and played music for the weekly liturgy.

Mato Grosso

In Porto Alegre do Norte, Sisters Jean Bellini and Maureen Finn were involved in social justice issues, living and working in the Prelacy. (A Prelacy is an organized church body led by a prelate that is a step before becoming an official diocese because it has few priests and no financial independence. This particular prelacy was supported primarily by benefactors and friends in Spain.) Maureen, as a member of the Prelacy Team dealing with Human Rights problems, was chosen to represent the pastoral agents at the Prelacy level. Maureen was also active on the Council in Defense of the Child and the Adolescent in Porto Alegre do Norte. After some serious internal financial corruption was discovered, she was elected Treasurer of the Council. Actually, the story is more convoluted than simple facts might suggest. A large, rotund man nicknamed *Bebê* ("Baby") desperately wanted to be President of the Council. However, when the vote resulted in a tie between *Bebê* and Sister Maureen, the outcome was decided by age. Because *Bebê* was a month older than Maureen, he was named President and Maureen was named Treasurer.[9] Ironically, this was a small coup for Maureen, because, as Treasurer, she actually had more authority.

Sister Jean was out of town participating in a renewal course of the Pastoral Land Commission (CPT) when she learned of the murder of three rural workers in Confresa in an ambush related to a conflict between squatters and land grabbers. Jean explained that, due to the proximity of this part of the Prelacy to the border of the neighboring state to the north, Pará, gunmen fleeing from the police there sometimes migrated to that corner of Mato Grosso, disguised as squatters. Upon investigation, Jean and the local CPT team discovered that the incident involved a showdown between two groups of alleged "squatters"—in reality, gunmen.

In contrast, Maureen's and Jean's daily challenges were much less dramatic, yet real: most of the medical personnel had left Porto Alegre do Norte, the doctor was unpaid for weeks and, sadly, the clinic had to close. But on an even lesser scale, there was one bright spot to be acknowledged: the last two kilometers on Main Street were finally paved.

MINAS GERAIS

In Uberlândia, Sister Maria José passed her entrance exam for law school, coordinated catechetics for three communities and participated in three Intercongregational Encounters for religious in temporary vows. As an educator and secretary of a local public school—in the poorest and most violent area of Uberlândia—Sister Ireny was active in the Conference for Religious, accompanied two communities, was the bishop's representative in the education forum in the Assembly of the People of God, yet still found time to serve as Treasurer for the SSJ Regional Leadership. On January 28, 2004, Ireny was officially installed as Secretary in the Municipal School System of Uberlândia, after having first passed tests comparable to a civil service exam and undergone a lengthy period of ongoing evaluation. In addition to this professional achievement, and at the request of Bishop José Alberto Moura, Ireny represented the diocese on the Religious Education Commission of Public Schools where she contributed to the education "norms" that had to be approved by the Education Department.[10]

Despite the fact that by 2004 the sisters were more involved in civic and social justice issues, there was time for plenty of celebrations and visitors. Sister Maria José made her profession of final vows in January, with her home parish in Cachoeira Alta praying a triduum of support prior to the big day, and more than six hundred people from her parish communities in attendance to rejoice with her. Later, many of the sisters attended the double wedding of (formerly Sister Regis) Deanna Sarkis' two sons. Her husband John Joe (formerly Fr. John Joe O'Connell OMI) was given special permission to preside at the ceremony.[11] And, of course, there were numerous celebrations of the 40th anniversary of the Sisters of St. Joseph of Rochester in Brazil.

CELEBRATING OUR 40TH AND BEGINNING NEW INITIATIVES

Visitors to Brazil for the various local celebrations included Sisters Janice Morgan, Marilyn Pray, Peg Brennan who had written the first volume of *The Good Rain*, along with several sisters who had already served for a time in Brazil: Sisters Janet Connorton, Kay Foos, Ann Lafferty, and Virginia Schmitz, as well as the return of Marlena Roeger after five years in the States for family illness. The sisters in the North and in the South were involved in the remote preparations. Both the Rochester SSJ Leadership and the Brazilian SSJs each agreed to sponsor one sister from Rochester to join the celebration, to be decided by lottery. A few of the Rochester sisters thought it would be possible to raise money to send two additional sisters to Brazil. Why not? Forty years is a milestone. Coordinated and spurred on by Sister Monica Weis, donations were solicited at every congregational meeting to underwrite the two additional plane tickets. Excitement mounted when the day for selecting by lottery the now <u>four</u> sisters who would travel to Brazil. From the list of sisters who had served or visited in Brazil, Sisters Marguerite Dynski and Virginia Schmitz were chosen. From the pool of sisters who had never been to Brazil and who would just love to go there, Sisters Joan Marshall and Barbara Olmstead were chosen. Once in Brazil, there was good fun and laughter all around—even a bit of slapstick humor at Sister Katherine's expense. For example, on July 9, the Community *Jesus de Nazaré* in Jardim Curitiba paid tribute to all the sisters, especially those who had accompanied them through the years. Sister Joana, who had previously contacted Sister Maria Elena in Rochester to see if an old SSJ habit was available, commissioned Sister Virginia Schmitz to bring it with her to Brazil. As the story goes, a young Brazilian woman, dressed in the traditional SSJ habit "imitated perfectly Katherine's accent, some of her famous *faux pas* in the language, and some of her funnier experiences over the years. The community invented a few other outrageous details."[12]

There were other official celebrations as well. On July 10, all seventeen SSJs went by bus to Itaguaçu where the "community of Our Lady of Lourdes honored the presence of all the sisters, especially Sister Barbara who [had] remained a constant in the community for more than thirty-five years." The community even created a video, describing "the importance of her contributions to the life of Itaguaçu." The next day, all were invited for lunch as guests of the mayor of Paranaiguara, and in the evening, Mass was offered by Bishop Benedict Coscia (who had initially invited the Sisters to his diocese of Jatai) honoring Sister Christel Burgmaier for her thirty-five years in Paranaiguara as nurse, social worker, pastoral agent, and contributor to multiple health initiatives, "with special mention of all the children she brought into the world." The next day in São Simão, the chief engineer of the hydroelectric dam built in the late 70s greeted the sisters with chocolates and flowers and "paid a long and eloquent tribute to [the sisters'] contributions, especially in the area of education." The engineer, himself, had been taught by the early Sisters of St. Joseph. [13]

Back in Goiânia, Sister Katherine was honored by the international NGO *Soroptimista* for her positive contributions to healthy lifestyle. Sister Ellen Kuhl engaged in more training to become a doula, accompanying women through pre-birth and labor, and Sister Maria José finished her law studies and began her thesis project: "The Community Council on Human Rights and the Penal System." She became more involved in jail ministry, handling complaints and contacting the families of the men and women incarcerated in the inadequate facilities. Maria José was also involved in the *Jesus Ressuscitado* community and participated in a program of the Conference of Religious for young men and women religious in temporary profession that was part of and sponsored by the Brazilian Conference of Religious.

In Goiânia, the sisters were accompanying several communities, and contributing to the network of congregations of women religious who lived in the northwest region of the city and who met four times a year to share ideas of ministry and to offer mutual support. The lack of priests in the area motivated discussion with theologians and liturgists about liturgical celebrations with presiders other than priests. Subsequently, after creating an agreed upon ritual, several of our sisters became the Sunday presiders of liturgy in their local communities.

Meanwhile, Sister Suzanne Wills was following up on her commitment to the indigenous peoples of Brazil. Officially teaming up with Sister Jacqueline, a French Sister of Providence, the two pioneers settled into a house provided by the diocese of Recife (2,700 Km from Luciara, MT, where Sue had previously served the Karajá people).There she met members of the Tuxá and Tumbalá tribes (7 tribes in that diocese), many of whom had lost their land and homes because of the hydroelectric dam and now had no place to live. Sue's special gift was her ability to meet one on one with people. In her new position on the Missionary Council to the Indigenous, (CIMI) Sue was asked to advocate for their critical needs. From her early days living in a hut on an *aldeia*, doing her own cooking, growing her own food, and providing basic medical care, Sue understood the importance of maintaining the dignity and integrity of the indigenous communities. As Sue often said: "This, then is what my work among the Indians and with CIMI is all about: PRESENCE, SUPPORT, AND HEALTH TRAINING."[14] Her new work with CIMI which called her to be an activist for their rights was a real challenge for Sue.

In other parts of Brazil, our sisters faced losses that foretold violent, fragile, and difficult times to come. Locally, the neighborhoods in Jardim Curitiba and Estrela Dalva were experiencing an increase in robberies that eventually led to closing the house in Curitiba and finding a safer residence for the sisters in Estrela Dalva. One incident in Curitiba precipitated the relocation. Sometime in November 2003, when Sisters Katherine and Maria José were with their respective parish communities and not home, Sister Anne Marvin was alone in the house. In her words: "I was sitting on the couch watching the news on TV with our new dog at my feet. The back and front doors were open as they usually were if someone was home. Four young men entered the kitchen door, at least two of them with one hand in the air holding a pistol. The dog hurried behind the couch. I stood up and with my best teacher voice said: 'I want you to leave NOW!' One said: 'and I want you to sit down.' So I did. They went through the three bedrooms, living room and kitchen" and found the box of bread money for our daily morning trip to the bakery. Of course, they wanted more—and I wanted them out of the house before Katherine and Maria José returned. "That's when one rushed over to me and put the gun to my neck and asked, 'Where are you going?' 'I'm going to show you where we keep the money' . . . .I took him to a small dresser in the computer room where there was a box with maybe 30-40 *reais* Brazilian currency." I was hoping that would satisfy them and—being the house Treasurer—not the stash of money I kept hidden with my dirty clothes. And what would I do if they wanted the key to my motorcycle?" Anne wraps up her story succinctly: "At this point they left."[15]

Some months later in the summer of 2004, while Sister Katherine was in the States, Maria José and Anne "scouted around and found a house to rent in Estrela Dalva and moved into it before Katherine returned. The new house, while a better living option, was farther away from Katherine's communities, which meant more travel by several buses for her to reach the Community of *Jesus de Nazaré*. Seemingly indefatigable, she continued her work on various Health Councils, was available for mini-courses, especially on the sacrament of Reconciliation, and was instrumental in creating a booklet; "Celebrations of Reconciliation Without a Priest."

While not really a humorous event, Sister Marlena, living in Goiânia, had all her clothes stolen off a clothesline outside of the house. Sister Joana, also living in Goiânia, was robbed at gunpoint in the center of the city. Because Marlena had just returned from the States, she visited every SSJ house in Brazil to discern where her gifts might best be used. After their January 2005 Regional Meeting, the sisters supported Marlena's decision to move to Uberlândia where she focused her ministry on the new rural communities springing up. She was instrumental in seeking free bus passes for the men who had jobs in the city and advocating for recognition of their legal right to land. Sister Ireny, also living in Uberlândia, had her share of witnessing violence. Because the Municipal school where she was Secretary was in the middle of gang territory and a neighborhood housing a prison, there was a drug-related pistol fight one day, right at her school entrance during which one adult was killed. All the sisters were acutely aware of the changing culture in the cities and the rise of violence precipitated by overwhelming poverty. For Sister Anne Marvin, the changes were poignant: adapting to a new rental house in Estrela Dalva, responding to the death of Fatima, a close friend and important lay woman in the community, and the slow disintegration of both the Parish Council and the youth group that Anne had been accompanying and encouraging. There remained a crying need to train new catechists for that community.

ACTIVITIES IN THE PRELACY

Both Sisters Jean Bellini and Maureen Finn were working in the Prelacy of São Félix do Araguaia in Mato Grosso and living in Porto Alegre do Norte. Maureen was serving on the SSJ vocation team with Sisters Joana and Maria José, as well as working at the prelacy level of vocation formation by accompanying six seminarians living in Goiânia. In her pastoral community, she was serving on the Administrative Team of the Community Center that was overseeing the building of an added dormitory wing for forty-two people. Her skill with finances enabled her to act as both bookkeeper and treasurer for the Center and acquire grants from various Foundations. Sister Jean's ministry with the Pastoral Land Commission involved participating in in-service programs on violence, labor, working conditions analogous to slave labor, documentation—all of which required days and weeks of travel. Jean spent her "spare time" translating and updating congregational documents, taking a graduate course in institutional analysis of religious life, and serving as Coordinator of the local Human Rights Center in Porto Alegre.

The Lenten theme of the National Fraternity Campaign (CNBB National Conference of Bishops) for 2004 was the importance and value of water. In Porto Alegre do Norte, both Sisters Jean and Maureen participated in a Water Festival that involved school groups, theater and catechetical groups—even a neighborhood celebration on the banks of the Tapirapé River. The water theme stemmed from a 2003 initiative of the mayor's office to privatize the public water authority, claiming the town did not have sufficient money for water treatment or stabilizing water pressure. With the question of privatizing the water again before the town councilors, the Lenten theme of Water helped align Human Rights groups, teachers, and community members into a successful "Wake Up, Porto Alegre" movement that forced the mayor and town council to withdraw their proposal.

Sister Maureen was not yet finished with her social action. She encouraged some of the councilmen to propose the appointment of a mixed commission to study the water problem and propose solutions. A group of three, Sister Jean and two men representing the civic community, were charged with studying the problem and proposing solutions. Ignoring the group's charge, the legislature officially approved privatizing water. The deal was done. Despite "Jean, in the name of the Human Rights group and Maura in the name of the Prelacy, [signing] a document...denouncing the process," the district attorney rejected their appeal "claiming that privatizing was the correct solution."[16] More civil corruption ensued that hurt the people: electricity was curtailed; bank services were blocked; garbage collection ceased; health units were closed; and many municipal workers were delayed receiving their salaries.

At the Prelacy level, both Sisters Jean and Maureen were involved in three significant theological and pastoral moments: the January Pastoral Assembly, the April retreat directed by Frei Carlos Mesters, and the November group therapy days directed by Regina Volpe. Nevertheless, after almost twenty-three years of living and serving in the Prelacy (1983-January 9, 2006—Jean for over twenty years and Maureen for over ten years) both Jean and Maureen decided to offer to leave the Prelacy. They sensed, after years of participating in the SSJ Regional meetings, that the inner dynamics of the SSJ Brazil group had crystalized. By offering to leave the Prelacy, the SSJ Brazil group could consider the possibility of forming new combinations of sisters in local communities together with new ministries, thus adding new energy and dynamics to the whole group.

CHAPTER 2

Endings and Beginnings:
Pruning and Nurturing, 2005-2008

THE ANNUAL REPORT for 2005 for our sisters in Brazil says this year was "calm compared to 2004." Plans were made and ministry/living assignments arranged. The January Assembly of the Brazilian Region, with Sisters Marilyn Pray and Barbara Staropoli representing the SSJ Leadership Team, elected Sister Maureen Finn as Coordinator with Sisters Anne Marvin and Ellen Kuhl as Councilors. After visiting all the places where the sisters were ministering, Marlena discerned that she should go to Uberlândia where Ireny had been living alone. She, Sisters Joana, and Maria José would be part of Vocation Outreach, even sponsoring a Vocation Encounter for fifty youths in Paranaiguara. The projected activities sounded as if the year would be off to a good and peaceful start. And yet, when one looks at the Annual Reports for 2005 through 2007, life was anything but calm.[1] These months were a time of endings and beginnings. Living situations changed; some ministries were concluded; new ventures were explored. Moreover, local and national governments were in transition or mired in levels of corruption. And their personal losses were significant.

LOSSES/COMPLETIONS

On the national level, Lula had assumed the presidency in 2003 with great plans for reform and social action, but his Workers' Party was plagued with corruption and financial scandals; in October 2005 voters rejected a referendum proposal to ban the sale of firearms, and in October 2006 the popular Lula was re-elected as President of Brazil, vowing to eliminate hunger. Allegations of corruption among politicians continued as did "terrible violence in São Paulo and Rio, directed by drug dealers from inside the prisons."

Sisters Jean Bellini and Maureen Finn had advised the bishop and pastoral team that they would leave the Prelacy of São Félix do Araguaia in Mato Grosso at the end of 2005, bringing to an end the presence and collaboration of SSJs after twenty-two years of service. They had raised the possibility that, in 2006, the sisters who were interested in exploring new places of ministry could begin to visit various dioceses as part of their discernment. During those 20+ years from 1983 on, eight of our sisters had lived and ministered in seven different places in the Prelacy, all small villages surrounded by rural communities. Sisters Jean and Suzanne were the first, followed by Sisters Marlena, Joana, Maureen, Dolores, Maria José and Elizabete.[2] By 1997 Jean and Maureen, the remaining two, were living in Porto Alegre do Norte, with Jean working in the CPT (Pastoral Land Commission) and Maureen ministering in various communities in the region. They participated in the meetings of all the pastoral agents of the Prelacy, taking turns as Coordinator of the Elective Assembly. But what was next?

Sister Jean went to the national office of the Pastoral Land Commission in the center of Goiânia and volunteered there for the first year, living with the sisters in Tremendão. Searching for a new ministry in Goiânia, Maureen connected with Habitat for Humanity and "learned how to lay bricks and put up walls."[3] She consulted the priest who oversaw communities in the pastoral region, and he indicated two small communities in need of a pastoral presence. Maureen joined the community of SSJs in Estrela Dalva and took a part-time paid job transcribing interviews for a degree candidate's thesis on "land struggles in Brazil."[4] Sister Maureen's good friend, Sister Mary Jane Mitchell SSJ, who had to leave her ministry in El Salvador for health reasons, was due to have serious brain surgery in Boston. This pause in official ministry was advantageous for Maureen who consulted with the sisters in Brazil and was affirmed to return to the States to accompany Mary Jane for this experimental surgery that proved to be a turning point in her overall health. While at first the prognosis was hopeful, Mary Jane declined over the next several years, going to the arms of God on July 27, 2009. Maureen was able to return to the States to accompany Mary Jane during her last days.

About the same time that Sister Maureen was absent, Sister Jean received word that her brother Martin had died in a car accident and went to Long Island, NY to be with her grieving family. While there, seeing her sister Patricia who was struggling with cancer, Jean decided to accompany her on her last journey and advised the bishop of the Prelacy that she didn't know how long she would be away and that her CPT team should look for someone to take her place. After Pat died July 30, Jean anticipated the date for her sabbatical planned for 2006 and made a thirty day retreat to further discern and explore ministry options. Both Maureen and Jean returned to the Prelacy for a time for some formal leave-taking in January of 2006.

In Uberlândia, Sister Ireny received the sad news on February 21 that her eldest brother, Valdir, age 63 and apparently in good health, had died. It fell to Ireny, as the eldest sister to inform her siblings. Sisters Marlena, Ireny and a niece went immediately to Cheveslândia, a distance of more than 150 miles, for the funeral for Valdir, a devout Christian and pillar of his local Church. Joined by Sisters Anne and Katherine from Goiânia for the funeral, the group stayed overnight in Paranaiguara and then, with several family members, returned to Uberlândia and Goiânia.

Word reached the Sisters in February 2005 on national news of the assassination of Sister Dorothy Stang, a Notre Dame de Namur Sister in Brazil since 1966, who was committed to protection of the Amazon rainforest and the land rights of the peasant squatters. One moment of grace in all this disturbing news was that the international outrage over Dorothy's murder encouraged the police to find and charge the two perpetrators with "conspiracy to murder an American outside the U.S." The two gunmen were convicted of the crime in December 2005, and sentenced to twenty-seven and seventeen years respectively. "The wealthy landowners, who hired them, continue in prison awaiting trial [as of December 2005].[5] Subsequently, the government unveiled a plan to protect the resources of the Amazon from encroachment, but the plan has been only somewhat successful.

Sister Suzanne Wills, living first in Paulo Alfonso with Sister Jacqueline, a Sister of Divine Providence, had been visiting several indigenous peoples in the state of Bahia, the northeast of Brazil, as a missionary for CIMI, a fifty-year old organization sponsored by the National Conference of Bishops in Brazil working to protect the rights of indigenous peoples. Sue was part of the first Seminar of Indigenous Peoples in Bahia at which 350 Indians, government and non-government, state and federal representatives gathered to discuss the rerouting of the San Francisco River. This event resulted in the formation of a permanent Forum of the Indigenous of Bahia. Shortly thereafter, in 2005, Sue was part of a March and an Encounter of fifteen groups of indigenous, as well as government and non-government organizations to contest the rerouting of the river. Petitions, strategies to revitalize the area, and the witness provided by the eleven-day hunger strike of Dom Frei Luiz Flavio Cappio, Bishop of Barra, Bahia, eventually forced the government to reopen the debate. In May, Sue was with her Tuxá friends for a "Mass of Remembrance" in honor of Xicão Xukuru who had been assassinated in 1998. Sue's involvement with the indigenous peoples allowed her to use her nursing skills to alleviate their illnesses, as well as learn from the tribal shamans the healing properties of various herbs and plants. Shortly after, Padre Alexandre from Ceará was elected the new coordinator of CIMI Northeast, and Sue was elected to represent her region in that assembly. Visiting the villages for the Tuxá, Tumbalalá, and Atikum tribes continued to take her time and energy as she witnessed each indigenous group's struggle to gain recognition of their land. But after theological studies in Recife and exploration about future ministry, Sue discerned it was time to leave CIMI Northeast. Not long after, she received the sad news that Bishop Franco, president of CIMI, had been killed in a car accident. The question naturally arises: Was it an accident? A carefully orchestrated assassination? Or?

There were more political struggles closer to the sisters' ministries. For example, Sister Barbara Orczyk, in quiet little Itaguaçu, had her hands full. As a member of the Community Council for Public Safety, she was invited to a quasi-secret meeting of leaders, politicians, and lawyers in the municipality of São Simão—of which Itaguaçu is a district—only to discover that lack of security was a common complaint. The one policeman who happened to live in Itaguaçu "spoke of the danger of working alone" to which Barbara countered: "and what about the people?" Thanks to Barbara's insistence, Itaguaçu soon had two policemen "circulating during the day."[6]

But Itaguaçu had other political problems that would directly impact the mode of living and economy of the area. The proposed construction of a dam on the Rio Claro River for hydroelectric power was vehemently opposed by the Association of Citizens of Itaguaçu because it would destroy the falls and the fishing in the area. Despite Fr. Anthony Boyle OMI' s mobilization of the people to save the "public Patrimony of the City" and Sister Barbara's participation in the Association, more than two years of public hearings failed to dissuade some town politicians and the developers. It was clear that the proposed hydroelectric plant would have a "negative social impact; the destruction of native and fertile land; the destruction of fishing; and no opportunity for local workers to seek jobs."[7]

A third frustration for Sister Barbara, beyond her primary ministry as pastoral agent and Physician Assistant, was the Tutelary Council for Children and Adolescents in the Municipality of São Simão. Eight candidates were willing to represent Itaguaçu, but the van promised to drive them to the location of the civil service exam never arrived. Once cars were arranged, the candidates arrived late for the test only to learn that candidates from São Simão had some weeks before received copies of the Statutes to use as reference while taking the test—but, of course, there were no available copies for the Itaguaçu candidates. Needless to say, there was no representation from Itaguaçu that next year on the Council.

NEW HORIZONS

But if life was not calm, and if there were many endings, conclusions, and ongoing frustrations, there were also new beginnings during 2005-2008 that signaled new energy, vision, and the work of the Spirit. The Fourth Latin American Encounter of Sisters of St. Joseph convened in Lima, Peru in 2005, attended by Sisters Elizabete, Maria José, and Marlena.

The Ninth National Encounter of the Sisters of St. Joseph in Brazil[8] was held in Maceió on the northeast coast of Brazil, at which Sister Katherine was invited to present a "historical memory of the encounters since these encounters began with her travels in 1979 in search of Sisters of St. Joseph in Brazil." The chosen theme was most appropriate: "Sacred Memory of of our Charism Incarnated Where We Live." Katherine's extensive travels, quite a few years earlier, to find and interact with all the groups of Sisters of St. Joseph working in Brazil was bearing much fruit—for coordination of ministries as well as offering spiritual support and theological updating for all the sisters. Not surprisingly, our Rochester sisters in Brazil were eager to see the affiliation expand and mature. Sister Marlena was elected as one of two representatives from Brazil to the Commission created to coordinate the Latin American Network of Sisters of St. Joseph. Marlena, who had recently returned to Brazil after extended family time in the States and was living in Uberlândia, met with the bishop, Dom José, about options for ministry in his diocese. One of his priests, Father Baltazar, invited Marlena "to work with him in the chaplaincy of Madre Paulina that attends rural and urban settlements of squatters." These groups were working toward agrarian reform, and also wanted to form base Christian communities. Eventually, there were nineteen communities that Fr. Baltazar and Sister Marlena visited. Under their guidance, the people were learning rudimentary skills such as preparing the altar for Mass, becoming articulate lectors, and training to be catechists for Baptism, First Communion, and Confirmation for the children.

Throughout these years, the sisters were engaged in Vocation Encounters, Prison Ministry Encounters, Encounters of Tribal Elders, and in their

July General Meeting, they discussed for the first time the value and feasibility of having Associates. Sister Ellen Kuhl's ministry was also expanding. She began offering craniosacral therapy in the new community center in the Parque Tremendão community and was invited by a colleague to open a space in a building on 20A Street in downtown Goiânia. The new office seemed like a good idea, but when the city site attracted only curious men, she soon, for obvious reasons, closed the facility! Ellen then returned to the Maternity Hospital as a doula and was delighted to be invited to write a chapter on Infant Massage for a book on maternal health.[9] Rochester Bishop Matthew Clark and his niece Grace Early visited for several days to experience "a little of their reality" and affirm their ministries in Brazil.[10] As Bishop Clark was fond of saying: "By definition, [your ministry] means to be incarnate in the place where you are."

In 2005, Sister Sharon Bailey, a nurse by profession, visited from the States to help Ellen with Infant Massage training. While there, she was severely bitten on the face near her eye by Capitão, the dog in the Uberlândia house. There was some fear that her eye might be seriously injured. After trips to two area hospitals and much delay, Sharon with Ellen, Marlena, and Maria José set out for Paranaiguara, more than 200 miles away, where Ellen and Sharon were planning to offer courses in *Shantala* (infant massage training) for mothers and caregivers at Sister Chris's parish. The return car trip for Sisters Marlena and Maria José back to Uberlândia was also fraught with challenges and delays: along the way they lost two tires, and the headlights on the car burned out. Marlena calmly reports: "it was almost midnight when we arrived at the house."[11]

Looking farther afield geographically, Sisters Marlena and Joana began translating for regional meetings and Chapters of various religious congregations that took them to many parts of Brazil and Europe. These first forays into their "translating ministry" expanded over the years and added welcome income to the community coffers. Still farther afield, when a 7.5 earthquake struck in southern Peru on August 15, 2007, the tragedy claimed 20 lives, injured almost 300, and displaced more than 39,000 people. Extensive power outages and damage to villages were widespread and long term. Because the earthquake and tsunami that devastated the coastal city of Chincha had occurred around the time that the Commission elected at the Fourth Latin American Encounter in 2005 was having its annual planning meeting, Sister Marlena and the other elected members of the Commission were nearby and felt obliged to view the disaster first-hand. The destruction and poverty were heart-breaking. Returning to Lima and the Peruvian Central House, the direction of their scheduled meeting was completely revamped. All of the Commission members felt the urgency to respond to the crying need of the people and our sisters in Peru. The conversation swirled around a common theme: "What can we do? We are always talking about supporting each other. What if we say: is there a way that every congregation in Latin America and the Caribbean can send one or two people to help?" As a result, the group challenged each other to send some of their members or volunteers to accompany the rebuilding of Chincha and the neighboring area.

Sister Anne Marvin recalls that, once back in Brazil, "Sister Marlena reacted immediately. She wanted two of us to go there. She asked the Rochester Leadership to pay for one plane ticket and we in Brazil to pay for another so that two of us could go to help out. Sue and Joana volunteered right away. However, Joana's passport had expired, so Sue and I went for six weeks" to work with the two Peruvian Sisters of St. Joseph of Pembroke who were alone in the area. The SSJs of Latin America and the Caribbean were sponsoring a housing project. We "visited the people who asked for houses to assess their situation and accompany those who were granted the houses. At the end of this time, we both knew that there was still a lot of work to do and that the other volunteers were all leaving."[12] Many people were still without adequate housing, suffering the trauma of the quake, and scrambling for whatever resources they could find. Seeing the pressing need for ongoing support and assistance, the sisters were faced with a difficult decision. Anne had just been re-elected treasurer of the SSJ Brazil region and, although she was responsible for the financial care of ten sisters, there were hundreds of earthquake victims. Anne remembers she commented to Sue: "I don't want to leave. Our hearts are beating to the same rhythm." But because their temporary visas were running out, both Anne and Sue had to return to Brazil. After much discussion among the SSJs in Brazil, and with the affirmation of the SSJ Leadership, and the knowledge of the C/SSJ Federation, and the Latin American Network of C/SSJ, Anne and Sue returned to Peru for a full year to form community with Sisters Maria and Gloria of the Pembroke SSJs and participate in their fifty-house building project by visiting families and assessing who was most in need of a house. When they arrived in Chincha Alta, Sister Gloria was preparing the liturgy for the Mass of St. Joseph "at which we four renewed our vows and formed a new life-giving SSJ community." As Anne commented: "I felt good, energized, and missioned." The last business Anne and Sue accomplished at the end of that year was to decide which family was to receive house #50. "It was hard to leave. We had gotten to know the people. There were still needs, and we were leaving the wonderful community experience of sharing life with Maria and Gloria."[13]

Although the idea may have been percolating in individual minds before 2005, the concept of a Central House surfaced in 2007 for group discussion. As Sister Maureen recalls: Every time we had a large meeting of the group, we had to pay a lot of money to rent a retreat center, bring all our papers and computers.[14] To help evaluate, prioritize, and set future directions for their life together, the sisters engaged the wisdom and skills of psychologist Dr. William Cesar Castillo Pereira from Belo Horizonte to lead them through a formal process of Institutional Analysis. After lengthy personal surveys, individual interviews, and reflection groups with Dr. Pereira, five elements were chosen as pre-projects to be worked on in teams: Central House assigned to Sue, Ellen, Jean; Community Living to be explored by Elizabete, Joana, Katherine; Vocation Promotion and Formation given to Joana, Marlena, Maureen; Financial Stability/Professional Work to be investigated by Barbara, Chris, Ireny; Mission/Ministries assigned to Anne, Jean, Maria José. A decision was also reached to research a location for a new place of ministry with Sisters Anne, Joana, and Suzanne volunteering to be part of it. The plan was to visit five dioceses over the next year to ascertain the feasibility of opening a mission there. The sisters agreed to explore ministry opportunities in the dioceses of Barra and Barreiras in Bahia, Cristalândia and Ipameri in Goiás. What interrupted this plan was Anne's and Sue's return to Peru for the year 2008.

Although all these new initiatives might have seemed to contribute to chaos, there was much to celebrate those years: several Vocation Encounters were held. In 2006, Katherine's 60th Jubilee and Marlena's 50th Jubilee were celebrated in various locations, as well as at the SSJ Motherhouse in Rochester; Sister Maria José graduated from law school and spent two months in Rochester visiting our sisters and learning English; the sisters living in Estrela Dalva in Goiânia moved to another rental property in a nearby neighborhood—Balneário Meia-Ponte—a larger house that could temporarily house the two communities in Goiânia while the house in Tremendão was given some needed upgrading; Sister Elizabete renewed her temporary vows at a ceremony in her community of Our Lady of Aparecida, followed by a great family feast enjoyed by all; Ana and Lindomar, an active couple in the church community, decided, after many years of living together, to marry, with Sisters Anne and Maria José as witnesses; a "Brazilian gathering" in Rochester in July of that year brought together many Sisters of St. Joseph and former religious, including the Oblates of Mary Immaculate, who had lived and ministered in Brazil; the residence nicknamed "house 22" in Jardim Curitiba was finally sold, and the sisters in Goiânia bought a second car to enable the eight sisters living in the city to visit their parish communities more easily. Perhaps the most exciting event was the translation into Portuguese of *The Good Rain*, the chronicle of the first 40 years of our sisters in Brazil, written by Sister Margaret (Peg) Brennan.[15] It goes without saying that the prayer and spiritual activities of the sisters were the underpinnings of all these events.

SPIRITUAL GROUNDING OVERFLOWS INTO MINISTRY

Most of the sisters accompanied one or several communities in their five locations in the states of Goiás and Minas Gerais. They concentrated on training lay catechists for bible study, offering preparation for Baptism, Eucharist, and Confirmation. Some, like Sisters Christel and Barbara who were medical professionals and pastoral administrators of parishes, focused on preparing laity who could offer spiritual support to the community, lead novenas and feast day celebrations. Sister Marlena, as a trained spiritual director, was invited often to lead retreats for Eucharistic ministers, catechists, Confirmation groups, and young college students. Several sisters completed Biblical Studies for certificates as Pastoral Agents, and the sisters themselves regularly took time for prayer and reflection in their small groups. They were also sensible about taking days of relaxation and vacation, as well as participating in the various Encounters for Religious sponsored by the Conference of Religious in each diocese where they lived. On special occasions, they joined with other religious groups in the area. For example, on St. Joseph's Day in 2006, about thirty sisters and several priests in the pastoral region of Goiânia spent the morning in prayer and then all came to the house in Estrela Dalva for a meal prepared by two members of that church community. In Goiânia, a special moment at the diocesan level combining prayer and action was the September "*Grito dos Excluidos*" march in solidarity with three thousand families in Granja, who had been expelled by the owners of the industrial park, relocated into two gymnasiums, and then relegated to provisional shacks. The sisters joined some twenty thousand persons for the long distance to raise awareness of this egregious injustice. It was a march of some 13 km (about 8 miles), but Sister Maria José insists it was at least 50 km (about 31 miles).[16]

When she was not walking in a protest march, Maria José participated in the Regional Encounter of Prison Ministries, realizing anew that the poor are not served well by the Brazilian justice system. For example, Maria José, with two other lawyers, produced many documents trying to resolve the plight of a poor lad, with no family or resources, who had been held in the provisional prison for five years, way beyond the time allotted for his case to be heard.

Sister Katherine's dedication to the various Health Councils was a direct overflow of her prayer and many years of commitment to the welfare of the people. Her famous dictum was a rallying cry for justice: "I continue to insist that a health councilor needs to have two special qualities: the persistence of the mosquito and the faith of the young David who confronted the giant."[17] Besides her medical support for the people of Paranaiguara, Sister Chris was involved in the Pastoral of the Child, overseeing four communities and some twenty-two volunteer coordinators and leaders, who talked to parents and weighed children monthly to see if they were gaining weight and flourishing. They also initiated food collections of rice, beans, and meat to supplement the needs of more than 200 families.

Indeed, the years 2005-2008 were not calmer than 2004 as the Annual Report stated, yet they were times of grace. That same grace was operative in the subsequent years of 2009-2012 that offered opportunities for leadership and two major initiatives whose seeds were already being planted. In due time the "good rain" would bring these seeds to fruition.

CHAPTER 3

Leaders and Risk-Takers 2008-2010

LEADERSHIP

"LEADERSHIP" IS A concept tossed around in business and government circles, yet it is essential in every phase of life. Books have been written about the qualities of an effective leader and online workshops can be found designed for every profession. How to be an effective leader was not a novel concept for our sisters in the Brazil mission, but in Brazil in the 1960s and 1970s, together with the Oblates, they developed a new way to lead. Rather than opening and   directing private schools for those who could afford it, they chose to work in partnership with the public school system, becoming principals and trainers of teachers for improved educational opportunities for their students. As the sisters branched out into the public health system, they collaborated in the local clinics and hospitals. They not only made their voices heard, but contributed to and influenced local, regional, and state policies. A cursory look at the Three-Year Report of the sisters for 2008-2010 reveals multiple examples of sisters not just participating in diocesan/regional meetings and Encounters, but being part of the planning process for these events, hosting the meetings in their homes, and receiving accolades for their contributions to the movements of a progressive church. The thirteen sisters—four in the state of Minas Gerais and nine in Goiás—had divided up their responsibilities and re-elected the same leadership team: Maureen Finn would be the Regional Coordinator with Anne Marvin as Treasurer and Ellen Kuhl serving as Secretary. Formation and Vocation efforts would be shared by the other sisters as time and opportunity presented itself.[1]

For sure, Sisters Christel and Barbara were and had been leaders for many years in their respective communities of Paranaiguara and Itaguaçu. Sister Chris, as a certified nurse, had been working full time in the hospital from 1989 on, training and supervising practical nurses and assisting the surgeon during operations and deliveries. Chris became the "go-to person" for all the families in the area. She continued working in the parish and had organized a choir for Sunday Masses. As early as 1975 Sister Barbara had returned to the States to earn her medical credentials as a Physician Assistant in order to provide more hands-on care for her families. Once back in Brazil, she worked in and became the director of the Municipal Health Clinic in Itaguaçu and later the director of the Municipal Hospital in São Simão. The new health clinic in Itaguaçu is named for her. In addition to overseeing the staff and smooth running of her clinics, she was responsible, as pastoral administrator, for nurturing the spirituality of hundreds of the faithful, coordinating liturgy, preparing for sacraments, training catechists, and initiating social justice programs. Both women were involved in raising funds and collecting food for the indigent in their area, as well as being present for significant family moments.

Sister Ireny Rosa da Silva, in addition to her ministry as secretary in the Municipal School in Uberlândia, was helping with catechetics in the parish of *São Benedito*. She was also coordinating the "nucleus" or core group of the Conference of Religious in the Diocese of Uberlândia, as well as representing the Catholic Church on the Ecumenical Commission for Religious Education. Her housemate, Sister Marlena Roeger, was part of the APR Team overseeing Social and Pastoral Animation in the rural areas of the Diocese of Uberlândia, coordinating the evangelization program in the *assentamentos* and *acampamentos* (public settlements and camps of squatters and landless families), as well as offering spiritual direction for some Junior Religious in the diocese.

Sister Maureen, accompanying the community in Brisas da Mata on the outskirts of Goiânia, spearheaded construction of a new community center, funded in part by small grants from the SSJ Ministry Foundation and the Little Way Association in London. In her work with the Conference for Religious in Goiânia, particularly their focus on environmental issues, she participated in the development and distribution of thousands of study flyers on the problems of material waste (trash), and the challenge of climate change to community groups and schools, and she prepared a presentation on the "Question of the *Cerrado*" (savannah, bioregion) for the national seminar. In September of 2009, Maureen was elected to the Coordination group of the Conference of Religious in Brazil to "animate religious life in this region" (Goiânia) and was able to take part in many on-going formation opportunities, including, on a practical level, learning how to use PowerPoint. She was also invited to translate a book for the Conrad Hilton Foundation, detailing the twenty projects they fund throughout the world. Quiet leadership, yet nevertheless, leadership.

Sister Jean, collaborated with the archdiocesan jail ministry team, making weekly visits to the state prison complex with a group of volunteers, and helping them to observe and report on the conditions in the three prisons. During their visits, some of the prisoners requested material for handicrafts. She found a local businesswoman who began selling bolts of string to the men and women artisans for their handicrafts, mostly rugs. In her work in the Documentation Department of the National Secretariat of the Pastoral Land Commission (CPT), she coordinated a team that organized, classified and prepared for digitalization over 380,000 pages of documents in the CPT Archives detailing rural land conflicts, the changing agrarian reality in Brazil, and the history and methodology of the CPT.[2] She also expanded an archival description for the entire national archive of the CPT. While not working directly with people in this ministry, Jean's efforts were significant in giving visibility to violence suffered by many rural families involved in land conflicts.

Sister Maria José continued her legal work for the prison ministry in the state of Goiás and was influential in several leadership roles. As representative of the diocesan Prison Ministry, she and a colleague, Gilene, were effective in calming the prisoners in the provisional prison in Goiânia

(CPP) when relatives of prisoners were taken hostage. On another occasion, she met with the Superintendent of the prison system about accusations of torture of prisoners by the prison director in the city of Morrinhos. Under the banner of the diocesan Lenten theme of "Fraternity and Public Safety: Peace is the Fruit of Justice," Maria José presented talks on the culture of non-violence, and met with Dr. Paulo Teles, the president of the Justice Tribunal about problems in the prison system in Goiás. She was able to document instances of overcrowding, inadequate pay and training of prison guards, as well as torture and execution of prisoners—both serious crimes, yet practiced by the Military Police. Maria José and colleagues also registered an official complaint with the Human Rights Commission about the torture of a prisoner by the vice-director of the prison in Itapuranga. Soon after, Maria José was designated by a Judge of the Criminal Court in Goiânia to defend some of the indigents accused of crimes, because the state of Goiás didn't have any public defenders at the time. She received a post graduate diploma in Human Rights, and in acknowledgement of her leadership role in justice for prisoners, Maria José had not only served as the Coordinator of Prison Ministry in the Archdiocese of Goiânia, but was elected for two terms as Coordinator of Prison Ministry in the state of Goiás. In 2009, in the name of the Prison Pastoral of the Archdiocese of Goiânia, she was presented during the Solidarity Fair of the Archdiocese with the "Dom Fernando Gomes Solidarity Award." At this same Fair, the Sisters of St. Joseph of Rochester received a certificate of gratitude for their participation in the work of Prison Ministry.

The name, Sister Katherine Popowich, was well-known in meetings of health care at the local, regional, and state levels. Katherine's persistence in advocating for equal access to public health services for the population that lived in the northwest region of Goiânia resulted in guaranteeing that a maternity hospital be built in Alto da Poeira, rather than in a more affluent *bairro*, and given the name *Maternidade Nascer Cidadão,* that is, Maternity born a citizen. She firmly supported the medical and nursing staff that prioritized pre-natal and humanized birthing care. Years later, the City Council determined that Katherine's name be added to the original name of the Maternity hospital. For her advocacy for improved health care, Katherine was awarded the 2010 Pedro Ludovico Medal—the highest award from the state of Goiás. Katherine's two special characteristics: the "persistence of a mosquito and the faith of a young David" were not only the hallmark of her leadership in health care, but also the incentive some years earlier for discovering and visiting all the Sisters of St. Joseph throughout Brazil and initiating the first National Encounter of Sisters of St. Joseph ministering in Brazil, held in Uberlândia, in 1981. This Encounter later expanded to all of Latin America. Indeed, Katherine embodied all the characteristics of a highly effective leader. Even the famous Stephen Covey and his "seven habits of a successful person" would have approved.[3] And Katherine did all this quietly, yet forcefully, focused on achieving a goal beneficial to hundreds of Brazilians.

RISK-TAKING

Certainly, the end of the first decade of the twenty-first century was a time of accelerated change and challenge for the world: the global financial crisis and protests on Wall Street; geopolitical tensions and rising protectionism around the world; the threat of terrorism at home and abroad; earthquakes and climate change; controversial development of the Amazon. In 2008, the first African American was elected as President of the US; and in 2010, Brazilians elected their first female President, Dilma Rousseff. Confronting problems and initiating reform required a certain degree of courage and risk-taking.

Living in this same world, the sisters, too, needed courage and initiative. There were nudges toward new ministries, new houses, and new ventures. Through prayer and discernment sisters were being invited to a degree of risk-taking. Not the wild, daredevil jumps of an Evil Knievel or the high wire perils of the Wallenda family, but the more theological and spiritual challenges rooted in the God of the Incarnation who risked taking on humanity with all its foibles—the same God who invites us to step out of our comfort zone, to take a leap of faith, and to trust the adventure. In the progressive 1960s, noted theologian Karl Rahner published an article on "The Theology of Risk," an incisive analysis of the creative response required in our fast-paced world. Rahner acknowledged that the Church follows a principle of theological conservatism to "preserve in truth and grace the eschatological fact of salvation by God in Christ." He continued: "Nevertheless, the principle of risk . . . is of great significance for the Church today." Rahner explained that "Risk here simply means the courage to come to new decisions drawn from the very being and mission of the Church, as an answer (positive or even negative) to the present-day situation. It means relinquishing old, tired ways and risking untried paths, where the future historical outcome cannot be adequately foreseen." In short, argued Rahner, the Church "is living in a period when it is clearly necessary to go forward with courage on to new and untried ground."[4]

Some of the risks and new ministerial paths for the sisters in Brazil were modest and apparently inconsequential; some more weighty—more radical—that required extended discussion and consultation, and even affirmation by the Leadership Team in Rochester. Nevertheless, each movement forward was rooted in faith and the courage to make "decisions drawn from the very being and mission of the Church."

Sisters Marlena and Joana, for example, in addition to accompanying their communities, began receiving multiple invitations to translate for regional meetings of the Sisters of St. Joseph Network in Latin America and Chapters of various religious congregations. As early as 2000 at a Latin American SSJ Seminar, Sister Joana had been invited to translate for the full Council meeting of the Sisters of St. Joseph of Chambery to be held in 2001 in India. Now, the invitations to assist as translators at meetings, conferences, and Chapters of religious congregations increased significantly. Joana's and Marlena's versatility with several languages made them a logical choice for this ministry, but it took them away from their communities for days at a time. For example, they traveled to Buenos Aires, Argentina, Concordia, Kansas, and the Sisters of St. Joseph of Chambery in Italy. The call to this mission was a challenge to each of them to balance community life, their pastoral commitments, and this new and exciting ministry.

Risk-taking was not confined only to the sisters in Brazil. Martha Mortensen, niece of then SSJ President Sister Mary Lou Mitchell, was interested in having an international experience to supplement her History & International Studies degree. From January to May 2010 she shadowed Sisters Marlena and Ireny in Uberlândia, volunteering in the *Pastoral da Criança* (Pastoral to Children) to see first-hand the game-changing work of Dr. Zilda Arns Neumann in pre-natal through age six care that had substantially decreased instances of infant mortality. She also had the opportunity to tag along with Sister Marlena to her rural communities, visiting homes and participating in a theatre program about the land issues run by Marlena's actress/activist friend Dagmar Talga. In addition to experiencing the joys and squeals of face painting, Martha was teased by the children into singing a popular song by Beyoncé. The children all knew the tune but wanted to hear the sound of the English words.

What stays with Martha even now, ten years later, is the hospitality of the Brazilian people and "generosity of spirit when everything is simpler." She recalls being almost overwhelmed by the poverty she witnessed unlike anything she had ever experienced. For example, Maria, a squatter, invited them "with no pretense" into her lean-to. It contained one sleeping bench for three people. Nearby sat an elderly man with only one leg, and Maria's grandson. Martha's silent presence and attention to Maria was what was important. Later, she could process the scene and weep. Such profound faith experiences forever changed her perspective on scarcity. Martha's question today about clothes and commodities is always "What do I truly need?"[5] For sure, her risk-taking immersion into Brazilian culture has born lasting fruit.

That same year, the sisters in Brazil continued to work with Dr. William Cesar Castilho on Institutional Analysis—a process now simplified by new equipment that facilitated simultaneous translation, thus allowing the Rochester SSJ Leadership to more effectively accompany the discussions. The focus was on the spirituality of the SSJ charism, vocations, and what a next bold step forward might be. Designating 2009 as "Vocation Year," the sisters made arrangements to invite Father Anthony Jacauna from Belo Horizonte and Sister Donna Del Santo from Rochester to reflect with them on vocation promotion. Study days were planned, three Jubilees were publicly celebrated, and sisters participated in Vocation Mission days in Cachoeira Alta, Sister Maria José and Joana's hometown, which involved sisters, laity, children and youth. They participated also in a day for youth sponsored by the Conference of Brazilian Religious in Goiania. Under the leadership of Sisters Marlena, Maria Jose, and Joana, Encounters on the topic of vocation were planned for three communities in Gioânia, Jardim Curitiba, Estrela Dalva, Panorama, and Paranaiguara. All the sisters in Gioânia helped Maureen with the Vocation Encounter in the Community of Panorama. "Sandra and Joana organized activities with children, Katherine offered a reflection on our Baptism as the source of our Mission; Jean coordinated the dynamics that encouraged a very good sharing on the vocations of marriage and religious life."[6]

For several years, a few of the sisters had been accompanying women in different cities interested in religious life. Now other initiatives were under consideration: updating the DVD used in the Diocese of Rochester for the annual collection for Brazil; development of a Portuguese website to be worked on by Jean and Maureen with professionals at DB SITE that was up and running by September 2010;[7] the availability of Skype in all the houses to facilitate communication; equipment for simultaneous translation in order to participate in SSJ Rochester Assemblies; and collaboration with the SSJ of Chambery on TV programs that not only highlighted the widespread problem of violence toward women, but also featured our expanded ministry with women in prison. The community believed that new approaches to vocations might inspire other women to join our congregation or become more aware of their unique vocation within the Church. Of course, nothing could be guaranteed; Vocation Year was a step into the unknown, leaving the results to the Holy Spirit. The two women already exploring religious life and living with the Sisters of St. Joseph of Rochester in Brazil faced their own moments of courageous risk-taking.

Sandra Silva Arantes had been testing her mettle in religious life by living with the community in Uberlândia and participating in several "*aspirinters*" (intercongregational programs offered by the CRB for postulants or aspirants or candidates).[8] In January 2008, Sandra was formally accepted into the novitiate and moved to the renovated house in Parque Tremendão, Goiânia, with Sisters Ellen, Katherine, and Jean as the Formation community. Accompanied by Jean as her religious life mentor and teacher, Sandra was exposed to new understandings of Scripture and eco-theology. Her ministry outreach called forth her leadership skills in forming youth groups in the *Santa Paula* and *São José* communities and guiding children's reading in the community library. She assumed the role of Coordinator of MAC for the state of Goiás, a program that focused on the formation of small groups of children and adolescents, by relating biblical values to their own lives and decision-making. The community rejoiced when Sandra made first vows on January 16, 2010 and was able to spend several months in the States with the Rochester SSJ community—overlapping with Sisters Joana and Ireny's 25th Jubilee celebration in Rochester.

Sister Elizabete Alves Gama (Bete) graduated from the Catholic University of Goiás, with a major in psychology after five years of study and an internship, while also engaging in pastoral ministry in the community of *Nossa Senhora Aparecida*. Accompanied by Sister Suzanne during her years of formation, that included several intercongregational gatherings of temporary professed Sisters of St. Joseph, retreats, and workshops, Elizabete was moving toward final profession, but, mid-year after much reflection, she decided against making final vows. After finding a job, her formal leave-taking from the community occurred in December. Her decision was both a personal risk of facing the unknown, and one that was emotionally draining on the whole community, for she had been with the Brazil community for thirteen years and as a vowed religious for eight of those years.

In addition to invitations for individuals to step out of their comfort zone, two big challenges for the Brazilian region lay ahead: starting a new ministry in a new location and the ongoing question—a kind of sleeping giant—of creating a new, larger house. The first challenge was an invitation from an external source, accentuating the ongoing tension between stability or missionary itinerancy. Is it more favorable to the mission to be rooted in one place for a long period of time, or better to engage people in new areas with a presence that can be transformative for all parties? What impact does each stance have on vocations? The second challenge was a perceived need within the Brazil region. Should we create a central house to address multiple needs and create opportunities for deepened community and new ministry? Each of the challenges required personal and communal prayer, regular sharing of the State of the Heart, research, discussion, and discernment. The next chapter, "The Theology of Risk in Action," delves into the history and context of each initiative, the steps toward discernment and decision-making, and the successful outcome.

CHAPTER 4

The Theology of Risk in Action 2009-2012

Progress in any human endeavor requires thoughtful planning, weighing of consequences, and, for practicing Christians, deep, sustained prayer. For the sisters in Brazil, the two challenges facing them were daunting: a) embarking on a new mission in a new geographical area and b) establishing a new or central house. Certainly, this was not a time for passively marching forward in the old patterns; rather, it was a call to deep prayer and discernment with a sense of detachment and openness to God's will. Specialists in risk-management for business, such as former astronaut Chris Hadfield,[1] offer tips for moving into the "unknown": develop a system for assessing the risk; move past a fear of failure; consider the upside of change; find ways to take on incremental risk; and seek advice from calculated risk-takers.[2] Certainly, all good advice, but the sisters in Brazil were more focused on responding to the movement of the Spirit. Their personal integrity, commitment to prayer, and experience of God's love quelled any turmoil, allowing them to assent to great risks. Echoing the thinking of Karl Rahner, the imperative of "the very being and mission of the Church" allowed them to say "yes" to the challenge. The story of each movement forward and its details is worth sharing.

THE THEOLOGY OF RISK IN ACTION: #1

The idea of starting a new mission had been swirling around for some time and came to a head in 2007 during the discussions and reflections that were part of the community's Institutional Analysis. Sisters Anne, Joana, and Suzanne volunteered for this new initiative whatever and wherever it might be, and the decision was made to explore ministry opportunities in five different dioceses in or near the state of Goiás. But this exploration was put on hold when Anne and Sue were missioned to Peru to assist in the aftermath of the deadly earthquake. About the same time, the Conference of Religious (CRB) in the state of Minas Gerais had a new project: an inter-congregational community of religious who could be a seed of hope among the suffering people in the Valley of Jequitinhonha. Bishop Hugo Maria van-Steekelenburg of the diocese of Almenara not only welcomed the idea, but suggested the city of Felisburgo as an "ideal place for this community."[3] Sister Ireny, who was active in the CRB of Minas, read about the invitation and passed it on to Sister Maureen. In 2008, Maureen, as Coordinator for the SSJ Brazilian region, participated in a meeting of the Conference of Religious in Belo Horizonte to discern the possibility and feasibility of our sisters participating in such an endeavor, and in December of that year, Sisters Anne and Suzanne went to visit the proposed location of this new intercongregational community. In February 2009, Anne and Sue were missioned to Felisburgo MG in the diocese of Almenara.

What sounds like a quick decision was in fact a process of deliberate discernment (with all due diligence) and spiritual risk-taking. Only Anne and Suzanne were now available for this new ministry since Joana was still finishing her studies in social work. As Sister Maureen wrote to the Rochester Leadership Team: "After consulting each of our sisters here (and talking with Sisters Marilyn and Mary Lou by phone) about the desire to be part of this intercongregational mission in the Diocese of Almenara, Minas Gerais, on December 30th, I informed the Conference of Religious in Belo Horizonte that Sisters Anne Marvin and Suzanne Wills will assume this new mission, along with sisters from two other Congregations."[4] The other two candidates were Sister Reginalda, a member of the Daughters of Jesus, about fifty years old and a member of their Provincial Council, and Sister Barbara, a member of the Missionaries of Crucified Jesus, who had been on their Provincial Council and previously had been part of the leadership of the CRB in Goiânia. Because Barbara was finishing biblical studies in Rio, she would not be available to join the community until a few months later.

FORMAL MISSIONING TO FELISBURGO.

On February 14, 2009, the sisters were officially missioned to Felisburgo in the name of the Conference of Religious of Brazil—Belo Horizonte region. As the SSJ Annual Report noted: "In Belo Horizonte a beautiful and lively sending celebration took place with the religious of the CRB and that same night, Reginalda, from the Daughters of Jesus, and Anne and Suzanne began a long trip by bus to the Valley of Jequitinhonha and their new house in Felisburgo."[5] As Anne recalls, the trip from Belo Horizonte, the state capital, to Felisburgo was a combination of waiting in the bus terminal and the actual bus ride—a total of thirty-one hours! With open hearts, they were launched on what came to be a fulfilling seven-year adventure. They were engaged in what Karl Rahner had perceptively called "hazardous venturesomeness."[6] This was new for us. With God's blessing, the new little community, representing three different congregations, discovered they could work and pray together easily and harmoniously. What a grace of the moment!

GOOD RAIN FALLING ON NEW GROUND.

Felisburgo, a mountainous area of village and surrounding rural encampments, has a population of about seven thousand. The inhabitants face many socio-economic challenges: widespread poverty, unemployment, violence, prostitution, drugs and alcoholism. The village has a main church, with three communities surrounding the center of the village, and six rural communities, including two *Quilombola* communities (people of African descent), and one of the *Movimento Sem Terra* (Landless Farmworkers' Movement). For many years, the people in the rural communities had lived and worked the land for large landowners who, some time ago determined they must leave. With the support of the MST and the government, these disenfranchised farmers have slowly regained some land, although they still do not have a legal title to it. The goal of their communities is to make a living off the land, gain title to it, and demand services such as education, telephones, and visiting health workers. Meanwhile, as a base Christian community, they pray together, celebrate Liturgy of the Word on Sunday, and pass on their faith and heritage to the next generation. In every way they share faith, food, and life with one another.[7] Their recent story, however, has been marked by violence. Initiated by one of the large landowners who had resolved to retake his land, hired gunmen invaded the community. Their local history is now "marked by the massacre of five landless rural workers on a November morning in 2004."[8] In addition to the dead, several farm workers, women and children were injured.

Although this violence occurred in 2004, the pain of the unprovoked attack lingers in the hearts of the rural farm workers. Much healing would be needed. Could the sisters play a part in that mending? Sisters Anne, Suzanne, and Reginalda would be the first women religious in the area. A priest, Father Davi, visited for Mass once or twice a month—when the rains permitted. Surely, the challenges were daunting, yet there was overarching support for the sisters from the diocese of Almenara through scheduled Encounters of religious educators, priests and women religious in the diocese. Thanks to progressive bishops, the hopes of Vatican II were firmly established in this diocese and in Felisburgo. The laity were well-trained catechists, liturgy coordinators, and leaders of their church community. There was some concern among the people of Felisburgo that the newly arrived sisters might be intending to "take over" the work of the community. But what the Bishop really wanted was sisters to focus on the rural communities—those who had been attacked and the communities of indigenous peoples in order to support their leaders. He hoped the sisters would assist the people in organizing liturgy, sacramental preparation, training catechists, and whatever else they might see as Christian encouragement.

Suzanne, Anne, and Reginalda wisely reached out to the people, observed, and listened. Anne recalls: "Little by little we began to know the parish leaders, participating in the Parish Council, in a meeting with the people of Bela Vista, and participating in the celebrations at the main Church and in the three communities (Bela Vista, Alta Capelinha, and Our Lady of Help) on the outskirts of town." In true Sister of St. Joseph hospitality, their little house was "always open to serve coffee and many times dinner and even a place to sleep for people from the [outlying] communities."[9] Anne remembers that they were a "perfect group . . .we just jelled . . . and were never strangers to one another."[10] Students from the rural encampment arrived by bus at 11:30 a.m. yet their classes didn't begin until 1 p.m. so three or four girls often visited the sisters while waiting for class. "Lots of times they ate with us and have even learned to play Uno. Throughout the year people from the encampment have stayed the night in our house and feel that our house is a place where they are very much welcomed and supported in their struggles." The diocese had agreed to provide a house for the sisters with the equivalent of one salary for basic house expenses and were hoping to provide them with a car. That first car, however, a '95 Fiat Uno, became its own story.

As Sister Anne wrote to Sister Marilyn: on one of our first trips to the rural community, the car had a flat tire. "Sue and a woman who was with us walked ahead to see if there was a house nearby. They went to find a man. Reginalda and I attempted to put on the spare. Using our full weight, neither one of us could loosen not even one of the rusted bolts. We prayed to St. Joseph and Mother Candida (foundress of the Daughters) and we removed all four bolts with a flip of the wrist. It seems that even our patrons in heaven find it easy to work together."[11] But, of course there is more to this story. Instead of waiting for a man—now that the tire was fixed—Anne and "Reggie" drove down the road looking for Sue and the other woman. They found the two of them relaxing on the porch of a nearby house, having coffee and delightful conversation with the wife of the farmer who was still out in his fields.[12] Leave it to Sue to strike up a friendship with everyone she met!

With the help of the parish, the city government, local construction workers, and the three religious congregations, the sisters' house next to the public market was enlarged to accommodate four people; an annex to the house made it possible for each sister to have her own bedroom, with the addition of a second bathroom and back porch. The front of the original house became their chapel. The townspeople were very accommodating, and when it was time to put the roof on the annex, there was a "procession of roof tiles one night after Mass" to the house from the church several blocks away.[13]

A PARADE OF VISITORS—AND CELEBRATIONS

That first year was filled with new experiences, challenges, and many visitors, the first being Sister Sonia, the Provincial from the Congregation of the Daughters of Jesus who was eager to touch base with Sister Reginalda, meet Anne and Suzanne, and experience their little community. Soon after, the city was involved in Carnival time. Anne and Suzanne were introduced to "New Life," the senior citizens' group, and Suzanne was invited to dance with their "samba block" that launched the Carnival parade. During Lent, the sisters spread out to the four points of the city, each spending Holy Week with a different rural community. The Lenten reflection groups continued by choice after Easter, with the sisters preparing a novena for Pentecost to be used by the city and the rural communities. At the end of May, the anticipated fourth member of their community arrived: Sister Barbara, of the Missionaries of the Crucified Jesus.

Each month in Felisburgo seemed to have a focus or celebration. June was a month of festivals. Sisters Maureen and Ellen arrived from Goiânia after thirty-one hours of travel to experience the reality of Felisburgo and hold their regional meeting. (The current re-elected team was Maureen as the Coordinator, Anne as Treasurer, Ellen, as Secretary). The visitors also were introduced to the *Quadrilhas* (a type of local square dances) which were celebrated by multiple groups: day care centers, youths, senior citizens, and the community of Bela Vista. Rumor has it that each of the sisters danced in the *quadrilha* of the Senior Citizens, although "Barbara worked in one of the booths during the Festival." The visitors kept coming.

Sister Solange Damiao, the current coordinator of the CRB of Belo Horizonte was eager to see for herself how the intercongregational "experiment" was progressing and share the good news with the sisters that Felisburgo was being considered as this year's site of the missionary experience for Holy Week 2010. That would mean welcoming thirty women religious to the area for an extended time; the twenty men religious would gather in Fronteiras where Father Davi lived. This scheduled week-long mission, sponsored by the CRB, brought sisters into the homes of these rural families, to help with Holy Week celebrations and to share daily life and be mutually enriched.[14]

Thus, the risk of creating an intercongregational community began and flourished for the next seven years. The other pending risk—creation of a new house—was waiting to flower.

THE THEOLOGY OF RISK #2   THE IDEA OF A NEW HOUSE

Although the first Sisters of St. Joseph of Rochester missioned to Brazil in 1964 believed they would minister primarily in education and health care, it soon became clear that their mission was evolving. Responding to the call of the Latin American Church, ministry was no longer centripetal, that is, focused on defined activities in one concentrated geographic area; rather, it had become centrifugal. The sisters' ministry was expanding outward to new areas of Brazil and new ways of being with and caring for God's people. Just as the early Sisters in Le Puy, France in 1650 were encouraged to quarter the city and discover the needs of the people, the Sisters in Brazil chose to live in *bairros* and rural areas where the majority of families were of the working class. In due time, they looked, consulted, prayed, then offered their skills in ways that seemed appropriate. By 2007, the sisters were serving in four states (Minas Gerais, Mato Grosso, Goiás, and Bahia). The cry of the poor touched their hearts as they responded in manifold and diverse ways: intentional presence with indigenous communities, advocacy for land reform and support for squatters, supervising health care facilities, training catechetical lay leaders, and offering professional ministries such as legal counsel for the imprisoned poor and massage therapy for expectant mothers and infants. No longer were daily activities performed lockstep with each other as in those early days of the Brazil mission. Now schedules had to be determined individually, and quality time together for sharing meals and prayer became a challenge. Aware of these difficulties, the sisters struggled to find a way to preserve authentic community life and offer mutual support. Ideas were plentiful, and discussion continued for several years, yet conversation kept returning to the idea of a Regional or central house. But where? in Uberlândia? Goiânia? What would be its purpose? Was just being together enough of a reason for the research, expense, and work involved? What other uses might such a facility serve? The process of coming to such a significant decision was lengthy and labor-intensive.

RATIONALE FOR AN IDEA

Beginning in January 2005, as part of their annual Regional Assembly, the team of Sisters Jean, Marlena, Ellen and Joana organized a process for reflecting on the criteria for such a house, various ways to finance it, and potential next steps. In January 2006, the Sisters discussed and reflected, identifying the pros and cons of establishing a central house in Uberlândia or in Goiânia. At their July 2006 meeting, the Sisters began an Institutional Analysis process of their ministry in Brazil that identified five elements of Pre-Projects, including the possibility of establishing a central house. In their January 2007 Regional Meeting, Sisters Sue, Ellen, and Jean agreed to work on the central house issue, but after lengthy discussion at the June 2007 congregational meeting, it was decided "not to open a Central house in the foreseeable future."[15] However, times, needs, and ideas kept changing, and the question persisted, yet changed focus.

The Sisters had, since 1988, "lived in two communities in Goiânia in neighboring *bairros* in northwest Goiânia (Nova Esperança and Jardin Curitiba). "Over the years," they noted, "we moved from one *bairro* to another, living in 5 different houses, serving 7 different base communities." In the first decade of the century, the Sisters were living in two communities in Goiânia (Parque Tremendão and a rental house in Balneário); two novices and a temporary professed sister needed access to courses and spiritual direction in Goiânia and Sister Katherine's health issues were increasing. Anne and Sue were in transition, waiting until they could leave to assist the earthquake victims in Peru and then later, waiting to become part of the intercongregational community in Felisburgo. By 2010, the praying, consulting, and candid, reflective discussion brought the sisters to a decision. It was a decision not based on compromise, but on their current needs for a larger house. "In talking we realized that, while attending to the needs of the sisters in Goiânia, we could also design a space that could receive sisters with special health needs due to aging and/or illness. A single residence would also combine and reduce certain expenses." Prior to this date, the sisters had to negotiate a retreat house for their regional meetings which meant some financial expense, as well as bringing all their computers, papers, and notes with them to the meeting. Sisters Jean and Maureen assumed the burden of research, contact with architects, builders, and fund raising, a project that would take many months of planning and decision-making. "In February 2011, we bought a lot in Recanto do Bosque, midway between the two *bairros* in which we currently live, a location that allows us to continue serving in our current places of ministry."[16]

There were many advantages to identifying a central location for one house in northwest Goiânia. As the sisters in Brazil communicated to the congregation in Rochester, such a house would provide "greater stability and visibility for the Sisters of St. Joseph who live and minister to the People of God in Goiânia; hospitality toward family members, friends, volunteers and young women discerning religious life; hospitality and service for the people of the faith communities in this region; hospitality to other religious women who minister in this region." Embedded in their formal proposal was the value of a single residence providing "mutual support and encouragement... as one community, to enhance their shared life and mission." Building a house on a new parcel of land that was properly registered in the town offices offered an additional advantage because it would bypass pending legal complications surrounding their present house in Parque Tremendâo. Apparently, those lots had not been properly registered when the parcels were sold by the original farmers. The proposed location for the new house, however, was in Recanto do Bosque, a *bairro* "situated midway between the 2 houses in which they currently live and near the communities they presently serve."[17]

FROM VISION TO REALITY

The vision was for a house that could accommodate all the sisters living in Goiânia and an "additional seven sisters for short stays (3-7 days), so we can host some meetings of the Brazil region." With the assistance of their architect, Ana Maria, the plan was for "a two-winged home with a multipurpose covered area joining the 2 wings . . . suitable for meetings, retreat days and other activities" with a "capacity for 25 people." The new house would also include handicap accessibility and ecologically sustainable features such as "solar panels [for hot water] and a retention tank for rainwater."[18]

The floor plan integrated seven bedrooms, five full baths, two half baths, kitchen, living room, laundry, chapel, storage room, office/library, as well as one room adaptable for individual ministries such as spiritual direction, Maria Jose's legal services, and Ellen's massage therapy. The innovative covered area joining the two wings could be used for regional meetings, family and community festivities. Finances were, of course, a concern, but there were three streams of revenue and a proposed fourth: sale of the house in Parque Tremendão (which they had owned since 1996); increased income from salaries, especially translation stipends, and limited savings; fundraising and grant proposals; and a hoped-for Bridge Loan from the SSJ congregation in Rochester. Enthusiasm was contagious.

The project was intended to begin in the second half of 2011 and be completed in twelve months. The SSJ Newsletter of July 27, 2012 provided a progress report for the Rochester sisters on the construction that included the blessing ceremony of the site in late January by Sisters Mary Lou Mitchell and Eileen Daly who were in Brazil for the annual Regional Meeting. Yet building projects are never without wrinkles and complications. The contract with the first mason had to be cancelled because he did not have proper documents for his workers, and the sisters would be liable for any mishap. The second builder, however, was making good progress. Nevertheless, those days were not completely filled with joy because the sisters were aware that Sister Katherine's health was declining. She endured several hospital stays, and in April, the sisters were with her during her final illness and death on April 9, 2012. As Sisters Jean and Maureen shared in the SSJ Newsletter: "The weeks after Katherine's death were sad for so many reasons, and partly because we had hoped she could enjoy the new house with more of us living together and no steps to deal with."[19] In May, Sisters Jean and Ellen moved from the house in Parque Tremendão—which they still hoped to sell—to join Sisters Maria José, Joana, and Maureen in the rented house in Balneário (rented since 2006) to form a community of five sisters anticipating completion of the new house in mid-September. Sisters Jean and Maureen had their hands full meeting regularly with the architect and builder and making choices about floor and wall tiles, sinks for the kitchen and bathrooms. For sure, this was a major project for them, requiring hands-on attention, while also continuing pastoral work with their base communities and the Pastoral Land Commission.

Saturday, September 15 was the "big move," followed by days of unpacking and organizing. Soon, the curtains were on the windows, "computers up and running, phone installed, furniture distributed, clothes lines organized." Thanks to a donation from Marlena's family, grasses, shrubs, flowers and fruit trees, vegetables and a grape arbor were completed by landscapers. Gifts from neighbors and various donations in honor of Pat Frisk paid for wooden benches in the chapel, the built-in kitchen cabinet, and a frame for Sister Mary Anne Turner's photograph of the blue heron flying over the Rochester Motherhouse grounds, a gift sent after Sister Katherine died. Once settled in, the sisters in Goiânia now could be the community of welcome they had desired. More than one individual uttered a great sigh of relief that the idea of a new house, an idea first tossed around in 2005, had become a doable project and was now, in 2012, fully operational: "a community of welcome, prayer, ministry, and new life!"[20] But, of course, life never stands still; it is always evolving and offering new challenges as well as insights into our frail humanity.

Sister Anne Marvin on her motorbike

Sisters Sue, Anne, and Reggie in Felisburgo with picture of Reggie's Founder.

Sister Maria José accepting the diocesan Prison Pastoral Award, 2009

Sister Marlena at Mass on one of the rural farms outside Uberlândia.

Lúzia displaying one of the recyclable shopping bags

Sisters Anne and Suzanne in Peru after the earthquake 2007-2008

Sister Anne visiting a family in Chincha, Peru in front of their temporary home

50th Jubilee 2014 - Brazilians and North American visitors.

Sister Mary Lou Mitchell blesses the site for the new house

Sisters of St. Joseph in Brazil - 2016

Sisters listening to a presenter at their Annual January meeting

Sister Jean's birthday celebration, April 2023 in Caldas Novas

Joana, Ireny, Marlena, Maureen relaxing at a nearby State Park

Sisters Suzanne Wills and Katherine Popowich

Brazilian Associates-Renewal of Promises, March 17, 2024, Goiânia

---

CHAPTER 5

Fragility Balanced by Strength 2011-2016

WITH THE COMMUNITY in Felisburgo now thriving and the new house in Goiânia established, it looked as if the sisters' ministerial and spiritual lives would proceed smoothly, but "smoothly" was not happening on the global scene. Why should life be any different in our mission in Brazil, a microcosm of the world order? In those years between 2011 and 2016, the news media were focused on the upheavals, instability, and fragile peace efforts among governments, civil society, and our environment. To name just a few concerns: the Arab Spring generated ongoing disturbances in North Africa; major tornadoes, typhoons, and earthquakes destroyed lives and buildings in the Philippines, China, and America, while the Colorado River flooded; the US-Iran nuclear disarmament talks ground to a halt; the US consulate in Benghazi, Libya was attacked; the Boston Marathon was disrupted by a bombing; Pope Benedict XVI resigned; Edward Snowden fled to Russia after releasing classified US surveillance information; Russia impulsively annexed Crimea; Europe declared a refugee crisis; Brazil impeached President Dilma Rousseff; and Brexit became a new dictionary word.

THE FRAGILITY OF HUMAN LIFE

If our fragile planet was now being more publicly acknowledged, that same fragility was reflected in the sisters' lives in their Annual Report in a section entitled "Deaths That Marked Us." Our beloved Patricia Frisk, who had been a Sister of St. Joseph in Brazil from 1984 through 1994, left the community, established a house in Goiânia and later developed cancer. The Annual Report notes: "All the sisters—especially Jean, Ellen and Maureen took turns accompanying Pat during her last months—in visits to doctors, treatments, and swimming pools, the movies, and parties at her house." Sister Jean noted that as early as 2010 Pat "showed signs that her cancer was progressing and her resistance was diminishing."[1] Jean talked to Pat about returning to Rochester for the last stage of her life. All the sisters supported Pat's housemate/partner, Suzette, alternating nights in the hospital. Sister Ellen accompanied Pat to Rochester for radiation in May, and again on her last trip in August. Jean remembers that "Pat's will power was so strong that, despite the pain, she went to Rochester then returned," and eventually traveled one last time to Rochester to enter the Mt. Carmel hospice for her final days. After her peaceful death on September 27, 2011, Pat's life in Brazil and her "passing were celebrated in the two communities where she had been most active."[2]

Sister Ann Lafferty, one of the original "pioneers" to Brazil who had served several stretches in Brazil (1964-72, 1976-83, 1987-90), returned permanently to the States in 1990 and, after fruitful years in ministry there, passed away at the SSJ Motherhouse on June 17, 2011. During the second meeting of the SSJs in Brazil in July, held in Uberlândia, the sisters made time "to celebrate her life with friends John Joe and Regina [Sarkis/O'Connell/], their son, his wife and daughter. It was an opportunity to reminisce about our early days in Brazil and the many ways Ann's presence was so important to us."[3]

OTHER SIGNS OF HUMAN FRAGILITY

On September 19, 2011, Ellen and Jean found Katherine Popowich on the floor and semi-conscious; they rushed her to the hospital. As Jean remembers that day: "her fragility moved us and we became aware of our own existential fragility and finitude." Since then, her episode of a TIA (transient ischemic attack) and Katherine's manner of dealing with it was, Jean recalls, "an invitation to me—to recognize how it costs to depend on others and learn to accept help when others offer it to me. Katherine is teaching me with her serenity, and I admire how she is processing the new challenges."[4] It was in that same month that Katherine was honored by the state of Goiás with the Pedro Lodovico Medal for her commitment to social improvements of the Public Health System. When hospitalized, Katherine was ironically experiencing first-hand this same Public Health System. "That experience caused her to rethink her many commitments and give up some of them."[5] The sisters hoped that the new house and larger community in Goiânia would offer her more support, but she died before that move could take place.

About the same time, Jean noticed that Sandra, a temporary professed member of the community, was becoming more pensive and then resolved to leave the Sisters of St. Joseph, which she did a few months later. Nevertheless, Jean believes that Sandra's time with the sisters in Brazil "enriched both Sandra and us."[6]

Even the community in Felisburgo which was in its third year of harmonious intercongregational living had an experience of feeling fragile and vulnerable. After spending December holidays together in Salvador, Bahia, with leisurely walks in the historic district, excursions to the islands in the sea, craft fairs in the square (loved most by Sue), museum and ancient churches, the four sisters, arriving home, "discovered that thieves [had broken] into our house and stole[n] two laptops and three pen drives. Result: many hours of lost work."[7]

Not long after, the entire community in Felisburgo was plunged into grief with the brutal torture and murder of a twenty-year old deaf mute who was loved by everyone, "always smiling and walking in the streets, visiting and helping where he could."[8] Sister Anne recalls that the city was in shock. All that natural beauty, abundance, and good will, and yet the deep roots of violence had erupted to damage the harmony. During that same period, Sister Anne herself had been experiencing physical pain on the side of her head for more than a year. Finally, the source of her discomfort was discovered: an impacted wisdom tooth that now had a cavity.

The extraction process was difficult and recovery much slower than Anne would have chosen.

FRAGILITY EVEN IN COMMUNICATION AND TRANSPORTATION

The balance between fragility and strength could be seen also in the enormous changes taking place in Brazil in the areas of communication and transportation. Sister Maureen recalls with a bit of a chuckle that years earlier when she and Jean were living far away in Mato Grosso, there was one phone in the town—one phone to be used by the mayor, the bank president, and the general public. People would line up to make their business and personal telephone calls. Because Jean was already working on issues of land abuse and had to make multiple calls, once she was at the head of the line, she would have to scream into the phone to be heard, broadcasting her sensitive business to all the others in the line. On another occasion, in 1995 when Maureen was waiting for a date to be sworn in as a Brazilian citizen, she received a message—not from a letter, telegram, or phone call, but—from a little boy who had come from the mayor's office. He arrived on a bike announcing that she should go to the State capital within a few days for the swearing-in ceremony. Once on the bus preparing for the more than seventeen hours ride, Maureen received a telephone call from the Mayor—this time with a message to return home because all the judges had gone on strike: "Don't come!" But it was too late. Maureen was already *en route* to Cuiabá, the state capital. Luckily, one judge understood the sacrifice of her long bus trip and "went off strike" to receive Maureen's pledge of fidelity to the Brazilian constitution.[9] Similarly, when Sue was ministering on the *aldeia* in Mato Grosso, she received a telephone call that her mother had died. When she called Sister Katherine in São Paulo to confirm the message, the audio was severely garbled. Sue rode twenty hours on a bus to Goiânia believing her mother had passed away, when, in fact, it was her father who had died. No one seemed to be spared heartbreaking news.[10] But, of course, today there are more telephones, computer messaging, Skype, Zoom, and, of course, "WhatsApp."

Those early days created stories of inconvenience and aggravation! Maureen insists with a wry smile that more time was spent on buses from Mato Grosso to Goiânia than on the three planes to fly from Goiânia to Rochester! Even the SSJ Leadership was caught up in the unreliable communication/transportation system. Case in point: Sister Barbara Staropoli recalls with a grimace that when she and Sister Marilyn Pray were in Brazil for the 2005 Regional Meeting, they were on a thirty-hour bus ride with Sisters Maureen and Jean to Porto Alegre do Norte in the Prelacy of São Felix when the bus broke down between towns. All the riders were stranded in the wee hours of the morning by the side of the clay road, slippery from the rains. The driver obtained a ride from someone who came upon the scene and went back to the last bus station to call for assistance. The stranded passengers soon received 2L bottles of soda and sweet bread, then a few hours later, individual containers with complete dinners for everyone, but—alas!—without any utensils! Happy end of story: a few hours later a replacement bus arrived.[11]

ALLOWING STRENGTH TO TRIUMPH OVER ADVERSITY

Too much fragility can dissolve or seriously strain a community, but with prayer and attention, new-found strength can foster growth, creativity, and movement forward. The Annual Report for the Sisters for 2011 and subsequent months signals just such a renewal. At their January 2011 Regional Meeting, Joana Mendes was elected Regional Coordinator for a three-year term with Ireny and Suzanne serving as councilors. This election was a milestone in our SSJ Brazil history because Joana was the first native Brazilian elected to this position—a sure sign that the North Americans were not essential to the continuance of our Brazil mission and that "Brazilification" was becoming a fact.[12]

The days and weeks for all the sisters were filled with busyness: accompanying their communities, advocating for land reform and justice for prisoners, and developing new sensitivities to our responsibility for our fragile planet. Maria José was occasionally appointed by the judge to defend indigents in Goiânia; Maureen's community in Brisas da Mata was able to complete its Community Center that included a chapel for reserving the Blessed Sacrament; Ellen resumed her craniosacral massage therapy, gradually moving her center of work to the northwestern part of Goiânia; Chris in Paranaiguara promoted relevant courses for pregnant women and supervised an increasing number of technicians and nurses at her hospital; in Felisburgo, Anne was working with fifteen agents in the Ministry of Sobriety, and Sue was training catechists for baptism preparation, organizing the women for making crafts, and preparing for the Festival of the Land and Waters.

Perhaps the most amazing sign of growing strength was an idea that germinated at the sisters' July Regional meeting: the Ecological Bag project. Spurred on by Maureen's work with conservation efforts for the *Cerrando* and her position as Vice President of the CRB Board of Goiânia, the sisters decided to invest in "biodegradable reusable shopping bags, as a way to motivate people (including ourselves) to limit the indiscriminate use of plastic bags to carry food and everything home from the market."[13] One side of the bag proclaimed "I'm taking care of our home, Planet Earth"; the reverse side displayed the logo of the Sisters of St. Joseph. The sisters distributed these free bags among the people in their various communities, and over time noticed a change in some people's habits.

Not long after, Sister Phyllis Tierney, the SSJ Coordinator of Peace and Justice in Rochester, spent a month in Brazil to better understand the major social problems in Latin America and their implications for our common mission. In addition to sharing with the Rochester SSJs her experiences in a seminar on human trafficking in Goiânia, she experienced laity-led liturgical celebrations, the challenges of prison ministry, and life in Uberlândia, Felisburgo, and Paranaiguara. Phyllis brought many of these reusable bags to the Rochester motherhouse for distribution among the sisters and our friends. Just another way of bonding the North and the South and our mutual care for Mother Earth—and a modest precursor to Pope Francis' encyclical *Laudato Sí*, released in 2015.

Over the next months, the strength of speaking with a larger voice was evident with many of the sisters participating in pilgrimages or marches. For example, September 7th commemorating Brazilian Independence Day with a military parade was also a scheduled parallel march "The Cry of the Excluded," focusing on the marginalized and those "officially" overlooked in society. On October 23, Sisters Joana, Maureen, Katherine and Jean, together with a few people from their communities in Goiânia and three members of CPT Goiás, joined friends and relatives of Vilmar Jose de Castro in Caçu, to celebrate his life and ministry on the twenty-fifth anniversary of his murder (See Vol 1 pp.140-146). Those who spoke gave witness to how Vilmar's courage and serenity impacted them. Promoted by the sisters and lay leaders, over one hundred parishioners in the parish of *Nossa Senhora da Terra* participated in the Ecological Walk on November 6. Then, on November 27, over 2000 people, including several of our sisters, participated in the *Caminhada Para Trindade* (Pilgrimage of Ecclesial Base Communities [CEBs] in Trindade, village near Goiânia), celebrating twenty-five years of the 6th Interecclesial Encounter of Base Communities that had been held there.

LARGE QUESTIONS OF CHURCH AND OUR SSJ MISSION REMAIN

The increased migration of rural agricultural people to the cities challenged the progressive theological/liturgical life that had taken root in previous decades. Sister Jean notes that in the 1980s, the sisters had the "full support of the bishops with whom we worked." Base communities and lay leadership were common, and social justice issues were acknowledged and championed by the Church. But bishops retire and die, and their replacements often are unable or unwilling to support the fabric of a progressive laity-supported church. Indeed, Sister Jean identifies two models of Church that were developing: one horizontal and one vertical.[14] The model that existed in the communities where the sisters worked in the early days—progressive in theology, inclusion of laity in leadership positions, and social action—was a horizontal image of church in which the whole community works together to praise God and improve life. In more recent years and in other communities, as more conservative priests have been ordained, there has been a notable increase in the number of communities that tend to be more traditional and centralized around the priest or bishop with the people giving quiet acquiescence—a vertical model. Whatever "Father says" is generally accepted.

A related question, that is ongoing and of increasing urgency, is how do the sisters fit in this situation? What does it mean to be inserted into another culture, and where do the sisters fit in the larger picture of church? There are no easy answers to these questions. Sr. Peg Brennan identified them in Volume I of *The Good Rain*, and no doubt they will still be relevant questions into the next several decades. What is important is to try to understand the many factors involved, maintain personal and communal integrity, and draw strength from prayer and the community.

Tossed into this milieu was Sister Anita Kurowski, a temporary professed Sister of St. Joseph of Rochester, preparing to make final vows. As part of her SSJ Formation Program, some experience outside of the US culture was encouraged. Anita was delighted to see for the first time the southern cross in the winter sky, and at the same time touched by the poverty of some of the people and the need for vigilance against robbers. The walls surrounding each house in Goiânia surprised her: "You can't see your neighbors' homes, yet you hear the barking dogs needed for security." Anita's six weeks in Brazil allowed her to make her annual retreat with Dom Rui (Fr. Duane Roy) at a nearby Benedictine monastery and observe the everyday life of our sisters. She tagged along with Sisters Maureen on home visits, with Maria José to services at her parish, and with Joana to adult faith formation gatherings, including a fundraising talent show with a lad in drag singing "I will always love you." It surprised Anita that, because people are working during the day, sometimes "church happens" in the evenings. Anita was quite charmed by a class in *capoeira* for youth that seemed to be a mixture of folk dance and martial arts, accompanied by a one-stringed instrument. Sister Joana, whom Anita experienced as a kind of bard and repository of folk songs, explained that the carefully choreo-graphed moves represented the years of enslavement by the Portuguese when the people were under constant surveillance. The "dance moves" were, in fact, a subversive action created by oppressed peoples.

Anita's stay allowed her also to experience other expressions of life in Brazil: a celebration of the sacrament of confirmation at a *fazenda*, the grasslands and ranches with cattle tended by Brazilian cowboys, a brief stay with Sister Christel in Paranaiguara when Chris was frequently called to the hospital to assist, and a long bus ride to Uberlândia and time with Sisters Marlena and Ireny. Exhausted from a day-long class in Portuguese, Anita appreciated the quiet evening with Ireny who harvested a coconut from their garden and, with her machete, removed the green skin, chipped away at the hairy brown covering, the inner brown shell, then shredded the meat, and made coconut cookies for Anita to take back with her to Goiânia.[15] The long bus ride provided time to digest the cookies and her experience of a different culture, as well as the ongoing questions facing contemporary religious life and the Church itself.

Fragility, balanced by strength and supported by a prayerful, deep spirituality will not eradicate essential questions facing religious life and the Church. Indeed, these questions are perennial conundrums for any-one aware and awake to the challenges of life and daring to hope. As the Sisters of St. Joseph of Rochester affirmed in our Chapter 2023 Direction Statement: "We are rooted in the Gospel and energized by our charism of unifying love. Attentive to the needs of creation and the human family, we acknowledge the serious challenges of our time… and strive to be a healing presence in our world."[16] Meeting these challenges can be accomplished only by grace and with the "seeds of hope" planted by the sisters whose shoulders we stand on.

CHAPTER 6

Sowing Seeds of Hope 2012-2014 and Beyond

....unless a grain of wheat falls to the ground and dies,
it remains just a grain of wheat;
but if it dies, it produces much fruit. [John 12:24]

The "Katherine" Seed

The name Sister Katherine Popowich appears throughout Volume I of *The Good Rain* and is sprinkled throughout these pages of Volume II. Sister Katherine was one of the first five SSJ missionaries who arrived in Brazil in 1964 and was a vital part of the evolution of our SSJ ministry in Brazil. From the early days of teaching in the *ginasio*, to spearheading educational innovations as principal, Katherine was not only witnessing to the Gospel, but also watching and listening to the people. The eyes of her heart saw the poverty and the possibilities. As the sisters became more active in their parish and local communities and began serving as pastoral agents, Katherine was adroit at using her pedagogical skills to empower the people. Under her guidance, church members became trained lectors, catechists, and lay leaders of the Sunday Liturgy of the Word. Moreover, these leaders were <u>very</u> responsible and could be creative when needed. For example, one Lenten evening in 2005 when Katherine's community of *Jesus de Nazaré* was expecting Bishop Washington to celebrate liturgy at 7:30 pm, no bishop was in sight. At 8 p.m. again, no bishop. A little after 8 p.m. and with a church assembly nearly overflowing, the lay leadership began the liturgy. Katherine, who was not present that evening, described it: "About

8:30 when they were finishing the homily, the bishop arrived. He explained that he had difficulty finding the church, praised their initiative and continued with the Offertory."[1] On another occasion, Katherine's advocacy was eventually fruitful. A poor man in the *bairro,* but not in their church community, was having difficulty getting the government to release funds to fix up his house. Knowledge of his situation reached the bishop's office, was passed to the Vicariate, and then on to Katherine. What to do? At the next Vicariate meeting, Katherine spoke out. She "raised the issue... of soliciting funds from some of the better off parishes. They came through. So on the hottest day of August, seven community members spent nine hours in blistering heat, raising the walls and putting on a new roof. Mission accomplished."[2]

Katherine's initiative and research skills also benefitted her church community that was decrying the few opportunities for the celebration of Reconciliation. In the Directives of the Bishops Conference and in the Manual for Rites of Reconciliation, Katherine found justification for celebrations without a priest. After consulting with a liturgist, and presenting their findings to "some 300 members of the region," the Regional Pastoral meeting organized a commission to create a Rite of Reconciliation and experiment with it during Lent, Pentecost, and Christmas.

In Goiânia, Katherine was instrumental in helping organize and coordinate the 2005 Regional Pastoral Council, considered one of the best organized in the diocese despite the dearth of priestly presence in that area. This same pedagogical expertise carried over to Katherine's involvement in various health councils. As an elected member of the Municipal Health Council[3] representing the Northwest Region of Goiânia, Katherine was active on two commissions: "one to encourage and help the some 54 local health councils that exist in the city; the other, to try to understand the flux of health care by visiting the various Units, examining financial reports, and collaborating in developing policies." Through the efforts of Sister Katherine and other members of the Municipal Health Council who took courage from her persistent voice, the council was successful on multiple fronts: issuing contracts for *only* qualified health agents; uncovering the actual, not declared, amount of the government debt; mobilizing nine Sanitary Districts to provide clout to local health councils; and improving training in humanized childbirth for professionals at the Municipal Maternity Hospital.[4]

Sister Katherine's sabbatical time in the States (2006) offered an opportunity to read deeply about the new thinking of Vatican II and its application to Brazil; participate in the SSJ Federation event in Milwaukee; attend the holistic "Women of Wisdom" program in Ocean Grove, New Jersey; and be present for several Rochester celebrations of her 60th Jubilee—as well as undergo two surgeries on her ankle. Arriving back in Brazil to a bigger rental house in Balneário, and with an ankle that was healing more slowly than she would have liked, Katherine tackled the challenges of taking three buses to her beloved community of *Jesus de Nazaré*. Sister Joana recalls that she would take Katherine by car when the car was available. Then when Katherine returned to Tremendão, Joana continued to accompany her, since Tremendão was a long distance to walk. "Even so, she walked several times. And when I agreed on a time with her and was one minute late, she would begin walking to her destination. I had to meet her on the way with the car."[5] Thankfully, for the City Health Council meetings, the Council provided a driver. By the next year though, Katherine reduced her presence at her parish community to times she was needed to facilitate courses or attend the Community Pastoral Council. For those events, someone would transport her either by car or by motorcycle to a local meeting in the community center. Her involvement in the Municipal Health Council, however, had increased considerably. Katherine's time was taken up guiding elections and reviewing financial reports; moreover, the diocese asked Katherine to represent the Health Pastoral as a Councilor in the State Health Council. Continuing to believe in her favorite David and Goliath story and the qualities required for success, Katherine maintained that, "we throw our little stones in the hopes to make some changes."[6]

At the pastoral level, Sister Katherine participated in the five Encounters to prepare almost thirty men and women from the community for the Popular Missions event in July to make home visits and encourage the people to return to the sacraments. Another visit to the States involved removing cataracts and two subsequent eye surgeries. It became clear to the sisters in Goiânia that, while Katherine's mighty voice was still influential in the health care area and revered in her dear parish community of *Jesus de Nazaré,* her physical strength was diminishing. She adjusted quite well to her new limitations and the assistance offered to her by others. It should be no surprise that on April 9, 2010 Katherine was awarded the Medal of the Legislature: Pedro Ludivico Teixeira "in recognition of your effort, competence and courage in the field of health, expressing the will of the population of Goiânia to show their esteem and respect for each one of you."

Meanwhile, the work on the new house in Goiânia was intensifying. The hope was that with more people in the community, there would be someone home during the day to support Katherine. But that plan was not to be. The second episode of ischemia, during Holy Week of 2012, also required hospitalization, but Katherine insisted she be taken to a hospital that partnered with SUS. As Sister Ellen recalls, there was a long line of people waiting for admission. Ellen managed to secure a wheelchair for Katherine who had been standing and waiting for nearly two hours. A sister from another congregation, who was a social worker on the hospital staff, happened on the scene, intervened, and got the admission process moving. Katherine was experiencing firsthand the lack of staff and service, partly due to the religious holiday, but also because the hospital was part of the SUS.[7] Ever the advocate for the poor, Katherine was spending her last days in a hospital open to all. As weak as she was, while in the hospital, Katherine continued to promote the public health system, distributing newsletters from SUS to the health professionals! Ellen remarked: "Katherine was concerned about people to the end."[8]

With the sisters keeping vigil at the hospital, Katherine, age 84, died during the evening of April 9 (Easter Monday), a few hours after being transferred to the ICU. The sisters were in shock—as were all those who revered Katherine's person and ministry. The immediate dilemma was that the sisters had no plans for a burial site. They hurriedly purchased six plots in the cemetery, *Jardim do Cerrado*. Sister Anne Marvin wrote to the Rochester community, describing some of the funeral details. "Katherine's body arrived at the church *Jesus de Nazaré* where she had served for 18 years at the exact hour that the funeral director said he would arrive—1 pm on Tuesday the 10th. This in itself could be Katherine's first miracle." But there were glitches. The funeral director had forgotten the candles, crucifix, and platform for the casket. His offer to return to retrieve them (with Katherine's body still in the hearse) was soundly rejected by the people. Anne writes: "The people would have none of that! They arranged two wooden benches in front of the altar and placed the casket on them." Her wake continued throughout the night, with a microphone passed around for sharing stories. Hot soup/beverages/snacks were available on a nearby table. People took turns praying the rosary and singing psalms. Some of the sisters went home about 3:30 a.m., but Sister Maria José and some people stayed all night, "waiting for Rochester to arrive." When Sister Eileen Daly, representing the Leadership Team, arrived just one hour before the Funeral Mass, the people were relieved: "All is as it should be now. Someone from the family is here."[9]

Sister Anne remembers that Sister Joana offered the greeting for Mass, Deanna Sarkis O'Connell (formerly Sister Regis) shared a brief remembrance, and thirteen priests, including nine Oblates of Mary Immaculate concelebrated the Mass. Oblate Fr. Jeremiah Donovan's homily summarized the impact of the arrival of the first sisters which included Katherine: "In 1964 we were expecting some nuns, but we got sisters." Exactly so. The Sisters of St. Joseph were committed to the values outlined in their early documents: "doing all that a woman is capable of doing." Katherine was a model of that ethic.

During the funeral procession, Katherine's casket was open with the "people surging forward for one last look. Huge bouquets of flowers from various communities" were covering Katherine's body "with the exception of her hands and upper body" (Eileen Daly) with some tied onto the top of the hearse, and the City Health Council provided three buses to transport people to the cemetery. It was the custom at the grave site to open the casket one last time. This gave Antonia and her husband, dear friends who drove from Uberlândia, time to pay their respects, as the microphone was passed around again. Sister Eileen had each of the ten Sisters of St. Joseph bless the body, form two lines to accompany the casket to the burial site and remain until Katherine, our sister, was taken to her place of rest.

Immediately, accolades began pouring in and became part of the Seventh Day Mass on April 15 in the evening. Fr. Marcos, a Dominican from Italy, cited three of Katherine's qualities: "serenity, determination, wisdom." Bishop Mathew Clark of Rochester, and a visitor to our sisters in Brazil wrote in the Rochester diocesan paper that "Katherine was among the unforgettable people I have met in my life… She walked among the people in easy and peaceful ways. She encouraged them, advocated for them, worshipped with them…"[10] In her email to the Rochester community summarizing Katherine's ministry and impact, Sister Maria José declared: "Sister Katherine was our Sister Pioneer; she encouraged Religious on life's journey and encouraged the participation of the people in social issues. She left us her firm Faith in the Gospel by her dedication with the church and the people of God… We thank God for the fruits of her life as a true Sister of us and our people." (Maria José)[11] In Rochester on April 28, 2012, the SSJ congregation held a funeral Mass for Katherine that was recorded and the video sent to Brazil on a DVD. Sister Mary Ann Mayer in her welcome described Katherine as a woman "who held God's people in her heart and gave her all . . . who listened to the stirrings in her heart." In 1964 she left Western New York "for Mateira in central Brazil where the roads were red dust—or mud—depending on the season . . . where the electricity was sporadic if at all. Yet where the people opened their arms and hearts to the sisters from the United States who struggled with their language… Katherine was respected because of her integrity; in her dealings with the people, she was loved for her passion for God, the people and justice, and her compassion for all." Citing a tribute from Irmã Elenice, Provincial of the São Paulo Province of the SSJs of Chambery, Mary Ann quoted that Katherine's life was a "constant and persistent search for God together with her sisters and brothers, in community, to help bring about the Reign of God, above all with the most poor and excluded."

THE "SUZANNE" SEED

In the years following the closing of Vatican Council II (1965) and the Conference of Latin American Bishops in Medellin (1968), two movements began to spread through Latin America: consciousness-raising based on the model of literacy training introduced by Paulo Freire,[12] and a companion call from Liberal Theologians to the Church, and in particular to religious, to *inserção*[13] (insertion). Embraced by the bishops in Medellin, this theological understanding was presented as the Church's option for the poor. Missionaries in training learn about the concept of *inserção* (insertion) and the kinds of transformations that individuals need to make to be effective and fruitful in the mission field. Simply stated, the concept acknowledges that by virtue of their formal education, religious rise from working class to middle class. When "inserted" into the mission field, however, the reverse must take place. Missionaries need to learn how to be an approachable presence in solidarity among the working class and the poor. If we choose to walk among the poor, we are invited to reverse the process and "insert" ourselves in their reality, without calling unnecessary attention to ourselves. To listen more than speak, to focus on their experience, not ours. This topic was frequently discussed during meetings of the Brazil Region of SSJs. Sister Suzanne Wills did not have to experience this transformation: from her family of origin to her time in Brazil, Sue never left the working class.[14]

Despite her training as a nurse, Sue maintained her innate unassuming manner, and the poor felt very much at ease in her presence. Her goal was establishing relationships and fostering community, a trait that characterized her thirty-five years in Brazil. Sister Joana, a native of Cachoeira Alta noted that "Everywhere Sue ministered, she left countless friends, *compadres, comadres* and *afilhados* (Godchildren). Whenever she returned to Cachoeira Alta, one of the first places she ministered, she made sure to visit nearly every family in town. At every house she visited, one more person joined her for the next visit. By the end of the day you could see a procession going with Sue from house to house!"[15]

From the early days, Suzanne felt drawn to be with the indigenous people. In the 1990s Sue lived with the Myky people and was spiritually touched by their "tranquility, serenity, freedom."[16] In her perceptive words, the Myky exhibited "Freedom because they are not imprisoned by time, by structures or by other self-imposed demands that make slaves of us. The day is theirs to do with as they wish, time to be who they are—no pretenses, no jealousies, no trying to be better nor to have more than the other." In the early 2000s Suzanne had moved to Paulo Afonso in the state of Bahia, and was living in community with Sister Jacqueline, a Sister of Divine Providence, the two of them accompanying the indigenous people. In conjunction with the CIMI (Indian Missionary Council) activities in 2005, Suzanne was involved in preparation for Encounters in the Indigenous villages of some fifteen different tribes who were protesting the "transposition" of the São Francisco River which would have seriously affected their way of life. Over the next many months, Sue made visits to the villages of the Tuxá and Tumbalalá people, had conversations with their leaders, and stood with them in their struggles for the land. But when negotiations with the government were delayed yet again and finally ground to a halt in 2006, Sue discerned it was time for her to stop working at organizing which was no longer life-giving for her. She needed to be with the people, not spending her time in meetings. With some reluctance, but with affirmation of her discernment, Sue resigned her duties with CIMI. Our faith reminds us that at such times of closure, a door of opportunity always opens. And open, it did.

After the 2007 epic earthquake in Peru, Sue and Sister Anne Marvin volunteered to go to Chincha, share community with Sisters Gloria and Maria of the St. Joseph Pembroke congregation, and assist the people who had lost everything—a relief effort that lasted for five weeks. With a strong sense that the people needed ongoing assistance, Sue and Anne shared their desire with the SSJs in Brazil and returned to live for another full year in community with Sisters Gloria and Maria. Soon after returning to Brazil, Sue and Anne volunteered to participate in another intercongregational experiment, forming community in Felisburgo, Minas Gerais, with two other religious, each from a different congregation. The new and promising ministry allowed the sisters to be present to the people in the various rural communities. Sue participated in an interactive Children's Pastoral and the Pastoral of Baptism, which was, as Sue said, "a vibrant way of bringing families together in a meaningful and enriching way." For Mother's Day in 2013, Sue arranged for a photo of each child in the Children's Pastoral, which was displayed and then given to the mothers. Consistent with her love for the earth, Sue initiated a recycling project with the women: covering bottle caps with cloth (*fuxicos*) and grouping them into coasters.[17] A collection of these coasters found its way to Rochester, and several sisters still proudly display them on their desks. It was well known among the sisters that Sue was always working on some kind of craft project when riding in the back seat of the car.

Yet not all was well with Sue's health. Looking back on their time in Felisburgo, Sister Anne Marvin recalls that Sue always carried a water bottle with her and seemed to be moving faster than usual as if she sensed time was running out.[18] When the two of them left Felisburgo on April 29 for Uberlândia and a few days of relaxation with the whole SSJ Brazilian community at a friend's *fazenda*, Anne recalls that Sue did not immediately jump into the pool (as would be expected) but was bundled up more than the weather required and had issues with a sore throat and nausea. This behavior was radically different from the first time they had enjoyed some relaxation days at this *fazenda*. Sister Jean remembers that Sue spent much time lying on a couch, mustering energy only for meal times. When they were playing a word game about events, Sue couldn't remember the answer to her question about indigenous people.[19] It was clear that Sue needed to see a doctor, and some persuasion was needed to make this happen.

Dr. John Luke (João Lucas), cardiologist son of Deanna and John Joe O'Connell in Uberlândia, ordered the initial assessment and encouraged Sue not to travel back to Felisburgo but to go to Goiânia for further tests. Ironically, the community she had lived with some years earlier at Tremendão (*Santa Paula Frassinetti*) and the community she and Ellen had begun were having their festival. Sue spent her days in Tremendão visiting people in the area, her friend Sandra, and going to the community festival in the evening, choosing not to share with the sisters that her first test results had indicated the presence of leukemia. As Sister Anne remembers, Tremendão was where Sue spent the last of her energy—among the people she loved and doing the things she loved.[20]

For the next several days, Sister Joana provided transportation for Sue to and from medical appointments. Eventually, because of increasing breathing difficulty, Sue was admitted to the hospital and eventually the ICU. True to form, even in the hospital, Sue was creating community. She wanted Anne to bring her slippers to her so she could visit the patients on her hall. And she prayed for the family of the woman in the next bed who had died during the night. After about two weeks of treatment, Sue's energy seemed to be diminishing. She developed pneumonia which made her breathing very difficult, so much so that she asked the doctors to put her on a respirator. Sue's good friends from many places came to Goiânia to be with her: David and Ana Célia, her *compadres* (the parents of her Goddaughter) from Uberlândia, Iramy, the mother of her Godson from Cuiabá, and her friend Fátima, a former Sister of St Joseph of Chambéry from São Paulo. The SSJs in Brazil all came from different places to support each other as they journeyed with Suzanne. Sister Joana alerted Sister Ellen to the seriousness of Sue's condition. Traveling a day and a half from Bertopolis (where Ellen was currently ministering) Ellen and Joana had one last visit with Sue. The doctor told Joana and Ellen: "tonight will tell the tale—either her body will begin to recuperate or not."[21] At 4 a.m. her body finally shut down. Exactly 22 days had passed from the time Suzanne was taken into the hospital to the day she went back to the One she served so beautifully, attempting to live up to the call of the SSJ charism she embraced: "that all may be one."

Sue's body was waked in the chapel of *Santa Paula Frassinetti* in Tremendão where Sue had lived in the 1990s.[22] The diocesan coordinator of the Children's Pastoral came from Almenara (near Felisburgo), a few *comadres* from Cachoeira Alta, friends from Uberlândia and many others from Goiânia. Sister Jean Bellini recalls that at one moment during the wake she overheard a "mild discussion" when one person from Cachoeira Alta said that Suzanne had promised when she "retired," she would live there.[23] Then one from Felisburgo contested, saying Sue said she was going back there, only to hear several from Tremendão said no, they were certain she told them she planned to move back and live with them! Jean remarked: "that's the way she lived and died: close to the people."

One can only imagine the heartache of the sisters in Brazil and Rochester and the grief of the people in Felisburgo. There was a constant refrain from them: "When are you bringing Sue back here? She belongs to us." The wake and funeral Mass with the Bishop presiding took place at the Church of *Santa Paula*. During the overnight vigil many people took turns sharing their memories, experiences and stories that connected them with Sue. In the morning a Communion Service was held in her memory, with messages sent from many different organizations and people with whom Sue had worked. People from Brazil and USA shared with the sisters in innumerous ways their love and support. Bishop Pedro Casaldaliga on behalf of the Prelature of Sâo Félix wrote movingly of Sue's deep spirituality: ". . . we are united in the Hope of our dear Suzana's Easter. She leaves a witness of simplicity and of her search in the service of God's Reign. From the Total Encounter to which she has arrived, we will follow in her path. With an *abraço* of fraternal communion." Sister Eudinea, coordinator of the Conference of Religious in Minas Gerais wrote of Sue's passion for the poor: "Suzana lifted up the cause of life and of life that is threatened, living among the little ones. She was a beautiful woman, dedicated and given to mission, a woman consecrated and full of God. Courageous, she accepted the challenge to be part of the intercongregational community in the city of Felisburgo, MG. All the good that she did together with the people to whom she was sent, she did with joy."[24]

After the final blessing sending Suzanne back to her Beloved God, she was taken to *Jardim do Cerrado*, the cemetery where Sister Katherine is also buried. As is the custom in Brazil, the Sisters and the community gathered for the Seventh Day Mass. In Felisburgo a Mass was also offered in Sue's memory. The distance from Felisburgo to Goiânia is so great that it was impossible for her dear friends to be present at the main services in Goiânia. Fittingly, their tribute to Suzanne was offered in their own town.

Two Sisters of St. Joseph of Rochester now buried in Goiânia . . . Two grains of wheat—seeds of hope—now put into the earth to bear even more fruit. Sister Katherine Popowich, age 84, April 9, 2012; Sister Suzanne Wills, age 69, June 22, 2014. Anyone who knew or worked with these Sisters knew that ample fruit had already bloomed because of their spirituality, their personal integrity, and their commitment to the people. The future will be witness to the "much fruit" promised by Jesus. We know that death is never the end of a story. Good Friday always gives way to Easter—and in some ways it already has.

New Seeds Sprouting - Brazilian Associates

Tertullian, an early Church Father, observed that the "blood of martyrs is the seed of Christians." Sacrifice brings forth new life. While Sisters Katherine and Suzanne were not martyrs in the traditional sense of experiencing persecution and death at the hands of tyrants, they did sacrifice their lives by living the Gospel apart from their native land and sharing the life of the poor—and felt enriched by that choice. It is no surprise that new life had already begun taking root in men and women who were inspired by the commitment and presence of the Sisters of St. Joseph. As early as 2006, the topic of welcoming Associates was part of the discussion at the January General Meeting of the sisters. The Annual Report for 2013 identified a group of women in Paranaiguara who met periodically with Sister Chris Burgmaier for faith sharing. Another group in Cachoeria Alta, where two of our sisters are from, began relating to the congregation in a more intentional way. But, as Sister Maureen Finn explained, every time the topic of formally establishing SSJ Associates came up, no one had the time to devote to it. Yet grace persists and seeds flower in due time. The current church situation in Goiânia is a case in point.

Because priests were frequently reassigned, many of the people in Goiânia minded the many changes and felt their faith was not being nourished. The trained catechists were longing for something more. Responding to this need, Sisters Jean, Joana, Maria José and Maureen began meeting regularly in 2016 with a small group of men and women eager to learn more about the spirituality of the sisters, their mission, and share with each other how they were living the Gospel in their daily life. Generally meeting on Saturday evenings every two months at the new house in Goiânia, fifteen lay men and women eventually requested to make their act of commitment for two years as Associates of the Sisters of St. Joseph of Rochester. The ceremony took place on Sunday April 29, 2018 in the parish church of *Jesus do Nazaré* in the community of Jardim Curitiba. Two members of the Rochester Leadership Team—Sisters Marilyn Pray and Mary Ann Mayer— were present to accept their promises and bestow the SSJ Associate pin on each. Sister Jean offered the homily.[25] It was fitting that a picture of Sister Katherine Popowich was on display in that church since she had been part of that church community.

According to Sister Maureen's report in the Rochester SSJ Newsletter, the "group is strong and growing! Four new people, a couple, a married man, and a widow . . . are participating in the program." The plan was to receive the new Associates after one year, and have the original group renew their commitment. They were able to experience a Seder meal in April with Associates from the SSJs of Chambery and looked ahead to the possibility of sending two Associates to the 7th Seminar of the Congregation of Saint Joseph in Latin America and the Caribbean to be held in February 2020. There was hope that a combined meeting of Sisters and Associates would help our Rochester Associates in Brazil experience the larger church and meet more of the Chambery Associates called *leigos e leigas do pequena projeto*—"Men and Women of the Little Design."[26] However, the Covid-19 pandemic intervened, putting local gatherings on hold. With few computers and poor internet connections, the group met online, most using their cell phones to share their reflections on various topics including Pope Francis' invitation to celebrate "The Year of St. Joseph" with the apostolic letter (*Patris corde*—With a Father's Heart). Everyone had a copy to read and those who could met online to discuss it. The group maintained contact through WhatsApp on their phones, and the Sisters, bearing boxes of cookies, reached out to each home during the holiday season. The Associates continued their various ministries of praying for the sick, preparing people for Baptism or Eucharist, serving as community treasurers, building houses for the poor, and offering free college prep sessions for youth and adults hoping to advance their education.[27] Once the Covid-19 danger subsided, the second group of Associates made their commitment in March 2022 and the first group was able to renew their promises. Again, by choice, the ceremony took place in a local church (*São Carlos Houben*) so that others in the church community could hear about and meet the Associates. Currently the group is meeting monthly and focusing alternately on aspects of the SSJ charism and social issues pertinent to their daily lives. We know that seeds find good soil in many places and take root wherever the Spirit blows them. Sisters Marlena and Ireny in Uberlândia are now meeting regularly with four interested women who, as of January 21, 2024, have become another local chapter of the SSJ Associates, one of whom is our beloved Deanna Sarkis O'Connell (formerly Sister Regis).

CHAPTER 7

Flowering at 50—The Anniversary Year of 2014

THE YEARS FROM 1964 to 2014 seemed to go by quickly. The Sisters of St. Joseph were well established in multiple parish communities, accompanying the people in liturgy, training lay catechists, and supporting social action. The intercongregational community in Felisburgo was a successful outreach and ministry with the people for seven wonderful years. However, the larger world in 2013-14 was dealing with tragedy and political milestones. The Boston Marathon was bombed; Malaysia Flight 370 disappeared; the ebola virus emerged as a pandemic in parts of Africa; people of Ferguson MO rioted in response to the police shooting of Michael Brown; gun control legislation lost steam in Congress; the Iran Nuclear Disarmament negotiations stalled; Russia annexed Crimea; Narendra Modi became Prime Minister of India; and the US Federal Government shut down for more than two weeks.

The sisters in Brazil, aware of these events, had spent time in 2013 soliciting ideas and devising plans for their 50th anniversary. Of course, there were other important items on the agendas of their official meetings. At their January 2013 General Meeting, held in the new house in Recanto do Bosque, Goiânia, Sister Mary Lou Mitchell from Rochester was able to update the sisters on various topics of congregational importance: the process and events of the Apostolic Visitation, LCWR's meetings with the Bishops, the C/SSJ Federation, the Diocese of Rochester and its new Bishop and the atmosphere of the Rochester Church.[1] Sister Eileen Daly shared the recent Chapter Commitments and the work of various committees, the current state of discussions on community housing, future of ministries, and future of the Rochester motherhouse. All these innovative directions in Rochester were not foreign ideas to the sisters in Brazil. Their Annual Report for 2013 indicates that conversation about new forms of leadership in the Brazil Region would be appropriate. A committee would work on this concept and bring ideas to their April meeting. Still, much of their time together was given over to generating ideas and plans for the upcoming 50th celebration.[2] The sisters agreed to a variety of actions: to remember in prayer the people and places where they had lived and worked; to visit each other's ministries for a celebration if possible; and to participate and plan for the "official" celebrations where each one is located. Sister Mary Ann Turner, who had served in Brazil from 1979-82, 1984-89, and again 1993-98, agreed to create a short DVD about the mission and ministry of the sisters in Brazil that could be used with the people, associates, neighborhood groups, vocation encounters, and celebrations of the 50th. Booklets about the ministry of the sisters could be printed with reflection questions to be used in "Encounters about our Charism" with various communities that the sisters accompany, and Sisters Jean and Maureen assumed responsibility for updating the website with a link to the DVD. Dates were set for the various celebrations. Individual Jubilees of the sisters could also acknowledge our SSJ anniversary. For example, Suzanne's 50th Jubilee, combined with our 50th in Brazil would be celebrated on Oct 15, 2013 in Felizburgo. Sometime in April or May, Sue and Ellen's 50th Jubilee celebration in Cachoeira Alta would also include the 50th anniversary of the sisters' mission in Brazil. They finally agreed that "official" celebrations of the 50th anniversary of the SSJs in Brazil should be held on October 17 in Goiânia, Uberlândia, and on October 19, 2014 in Paranaiguara. Paranaiguara, the first foundation (originally named Mateira) would be the most elaborate celebration with nearby communities invited. The ten sisters also agreed to prepare for this event by taking some retreat time and days of vacation together.[3]

Similar to the fortieth anniversary, the sisters in Brazil and the Rochester congregation committed to sponsoring one sister each from North America who had served in or visited Brazil—to be selected by lottery—to attend the celebration. An *ad hoc* travel fund initiated by Sister Monica Weis was successful in underwriting two additional sisters who wished to visit Brazil for the first time. Even though prices for air travel had now increased, the combined Brazil/ Congregational fund and the *ad hoc* Rochester fund-raising-challenge once again enabled four sisters from North America (in addition to Sisters Eileen Daly and Marilyn Pray from the SSJ Leadership) to enjoy the festivities of the fiftieth. Lottery winners were Sisters Donna DelSanto and Sharon Bailey who had visited Brazil before and first-timers Sisters Monica Weis and Beth Sutter who were eager for the South American adventure.

THE THREE CELEBRATIONS

The first celebration of our 50th year in Brazil took place in Goiânia in early January 2014 at the time of our Regional Assembly with all of our sisters present. Although the sisters in Goiânia relate to many different church communities in different *barrios*, they decided this celebration and Mass would take place in Estrela Dalva, in the *Resurrection de Jesus* community where Sister Maria José is very involved. A Mass was celebrated by Fr. Tom Murphy, Oblate and longtime friend and pastor Fr. Rogerio, and Dom Antônio Riberio, retired bishop of the Archdiocese of Goiânia. Many lay people and sisters were involved in the liturgy, and the community welcomed all to supper in the church after the Mass. The year-long celebration of the first 50 years of the Sisters of St. Joseph in Brazil had begun!

October 17 and 19 were devoted to the celebrations in Uberlândia and Paranaiguara. Guests from the States and the busload that came from Felisburgo were housed in rented hostel space owned by the Franciscan Sisters. Sisters Maureen, Marlena, and Ireny supplied breakfast food for the group, and after the Mass celebrated by Bishop Paulo Francisco, Padre Baltazar, chaplain of the Capelania of Santa Paulina which ministers to the rural *Assentamentos,* and Fr. Tom Murphy OMI, the parish provided finger food and time for reminiscing. Several sisters and lay friends had scrap books of pictures that everyone, including dear friends Antonia and Vincente, enjoyed looking at. Traveling on her own to the celebration, at the insistence of her Brazil friends, was Judith McKay, formerly Sister Jogues, who had served in Brazil from 1965-72. Reconnecting with her former colleagues and the families she had been close to was a transformational experience resulting in a new sense of joy and wholeness. Moreover, she discovered that her facility with Portuguese had not faded!

Over the next few days, the North Americans were treated to a sumptuous meal by John Joe and Deanna (formerly Sister Regis) O'Connell, as well as a supper of local foods on another evening hosted by Ana Celia and David Bagnel—with more stories and reminiscences. In addition, the sisters benefitted from a tour of the urban land occupations and Mass at one of the rural farms. A highlight of the week was a traditional *churrasco* (BBQ) at a *fazenda* outside Uberlândia hosted by Toninho, a lawyer, who proudly claimed he had been "reared by the SSJs and Oblates as a little child in *Bom Jesus.*" In keeping with Brazilian hospitality, Toninho had invited all the neighbors and community leaders to this feast in honor of the sisters and their transforming effect on the various small communities.

Another treasured side trip was a personal tour led by Sister Barbara Orczyk, returning to Brazil for the 50th festivities. She proudly pointed out the village of Itaguaçu, its famous waterfalls, and the new Municipal Health clinic now named for her. Arriving in Brazil in 1968, Barbara was at first a teacher and principal and then pastoral agent and social activist. Seeing the urgent need for qualified health care professionals, she returned to the States in 1975 or 76 to earn her Physician Assistant certification, so that she could be a positive force for improving health care in the area, becoming Director of the Municipal Hospital in São Simão. In addition to these significant contributions, Barbara was also active in parish activities and parish administrator in Itaguaçu from 2000-2010 with special permission from Rome to officiate at weddings and baptism, as well as preside at Communion Services on Sundays.[4]

To keep the party going, the group now moved on to the third celebration in Paranaiguara on October 18 where, as Sister Christel Burgmaier remarked, "we all started." Chris had arranged for visitors to stay with local families who loved having the sisters in their homes, and Chris was particularly pleased that the planning group had involved participation from priests, town leaders, parishioners, and many, many volunteers. The original town of Mateira, where the sisters first lived, had been flooded in 1975/76 to make room for a dam. Its geographic successor, Paranaiguara, was a carefully planned community. Through the efforts of Fr. Jeremiah Donovan OMI and the mayor, the entire central square was given to the church, with maintenance to be provided by the town whose offices were at the opposite end of this sizable land parcel.[5] To the North American visitor, the geographical layout was reminiscent of a New England village commons of several centuries ago. The many buses and cars of the visitors were parked at a depot outside the town, with bathroom facilities there and food available for the weary travelers. The busload from Felisburgo, including Sisters Donna DelSanto and Sharon Bailey who had flown from the States to Porto Seguro to join the people in Felisburgo, traveled over sixteen hours by bus to be present for the Mass and celebration in Paranaiguara. When the North American "delegation" arrived from Uberlândia by car (three and a half hours) the excitement in the air was palpable. The long-anticipated fiftieth anniversary festival could begin. The Mass was celebrated by Fr. Jeremiah Donovan OMI, assisted by Fr. Tom O'Shea OMI, Dom Rui OSB (a monk originally from Kansas but living in their monastery in Mineiros), and Fr. Neilton Nunes Neves (a diocesan priest who grew up in Paranaiguara.). To add to the festivities, the Sisters of St. Joseph (about a dozen) and the children were invited to participate in the entrance procession. With the parish ladies fussing over the order of the lineup, each sister was escorted down the aisle by a well-rehearsed child in her "Sunday best" and sprouting a pair of angel wings. Sister Christel Burgmaier coordinated the festive music, playing keyboard and directing the expanded choir. Sister Mary Ann Mayer, representing the SSJs of Rochester, offered the Welcome in Portuguese, and at the end of the ceremony, each sister was given a gift: a floral box containing a hand towel with crocheted edges and the sister's name cross stitched on it.[6]

The delicious meal after the Mass was overwhelming in variety and quantity. Donations of cows, chickens, and rice from farmers and ranchers had been keeping the women in the parish hall busy preparing a meal for more than 300 people. Volunteers did some of the cooking in their homes; others prepared main dishes in the community center kitchen—frequently taking a break to welcome the sisters from the north. Theirs was more than ordinary hospitality. The people expressed their gratitude for the presence of the sisters by embracing them and kissing their hands. The difference in language was no impediment! The hospitality continued with most of the North Americans and other visitors gathering at Sister Chris' house the next morning for breakfast, with Sister Mary Ann Coughlin (in Brazil from 1968-72) holding forth in both English and Portuguese. People were gathered inside and outside the house in Chris' big yard, chatting, enjoying pastries, and not wanting the warm feelings of communion to evaporate.

The two celebrations attended by the North American visitors—Uber-lândia and Paranaiguara—were very different in style, yet offered poignant and unique experiences. Although a big city, the Uberlândia ceremony was a celebration within base communities clustered in the midst of the bustling city. Because of ongoing migration to the city, not all the people knew the sisters, just the parishioners of *Bom Jesus* and the folks from the rural *Assentamentos* where Marlene ministers. This celebration could be compared to a village festival within the larger, surrounding city. By way of contrast, the celebration in Paranaiguara was a total involvement of sisters, priests, citizens, and founders of the town that became an official historic event, demonstrating genuine community. Furthermore, the Oblates, visible at both celebrations, conveyed the enthusiasm of Vatican II and what "church" could be. Although departures are always sad, memories sustained everyone's hopes and joys. Yet this trip to Brazil could not be complete without a visit to *Jardim do Cerrado* to pray at the graves of Sisters Katherine Popowich and Suzanne Wills—who had died just 3 1/2 months before.

CHAPTER 8

Striving for the 'More' 2014-2024

"Once the seed of faith takes root,
it cannot be blown away,
even by the strongest wind—
Now that's a blessing." – Rumi

THE EXCITEMENT OF the 50th celebrations continued for some weeks after the festivities, but the demands of daily life soon took precedence. Nevertheless, every day was not all activity. The sisters have always been deeply committed to prayer and spiritual renewal. They have consistently responded to opportunities for summer theology courses, seminars on spirituality and ecology, church-sponsored pilgrimages, national encounters, conferences, retreat times together and alone, knowing that, to be fruitful, activity must be grounded in prayer and contemplation. Occasionally they make retreat together. Communal discernment forms an integral part of their discussions in the annual January Regional Assemblies, built on each sister's sharing of her personal insights. Furthermore, they have participated in the preparation days for the General Chapters of the Sisters of St. Joseph in Rochester via Zoom and in person, most especially in 2015 and 2019. In 2023, almost all of the sisters in Brazil were able to be present in Rochester to take part in the Discernment Chapter of Affairs and the Chapter of Elections.

The sisters' ministry in 2014-2022 continued against a backdrop of a few positive world happenings such as the Paris Climate Accord and the

Columbia Peace Agreement but also some more terrifying events: the Russian intervention in Syria and interference in the 2016 United States presidential election; the destruction of Notre Dame Cathedral; the more than 80,000 fires in the Amazon; intensifying global warming and climate change reports; and the "Year of Protests" in Hong Kong, Algeria, Sudan, Chili, Lebanon, and Iran. Within Brazil itself, there were momentous changes: Dilma Rousseff won a second term as president (October 2014) only to be removed from office two years later (August 2016); the Zika virus, declared a global public health emergency by the World Health Organization, was concentrated in Brazil. Despite this health challenge, the Olympic Games were held in Rio de Janeiro in August of 2016. That same year, former President Lula da Silva was imprisoned for corruption,[1] and in October 2018, far-right candidate Jair Bolsonaro won the presidential election, but he himself became the center of controversy in 2020 by refusing to support measures to halt the spread of the Covid-19 virus.

Meanwhile, the sisters continued their commitment to prayer and ministry. Indeed, such grounding in deep prayer sustained their energy as they continued to be an intentional presence among the people, accompanying several small Christian communities in Goiânia, Uberlândia, Paranaiguara, and Felisburgo. Not surprisingly, over these years, there were numerous occasions to stretch that presence by responding to what Sisters of St. Joseph identify as a "call to the 'more.'" In small and not so small ways, a call to the 'more' involves the kind of risk-taking described in Chapter 3 that theologian Karl Rahner believes is part of "the very being and mission of the Church." Indeed, each day was a new invitation to say "yes."

STRETCHING OUR PRESENCE

GOIÂNIA

In Goiânia, for example, Sister Joana was elected to a two-year term on the Municipal Health Council which involved daily monitoring health policies and resources—and then chosen as President of this Council for two years. She also responded to several translating invitations including Le Puy, France, seeing for the first time the original 1650 foundation of the Sisters of St. Joseph. Sister Maria José transitioned from six years of coordinating the archdiocesan prison ministry to being its advisor, spent six months in Rochester refining her facility in English, and was often seen walking—by choice—the five miles between her language class at Nazareth College (now University) and Blessed Sacrament Convent where she was living. Once back in Brazil, Maria José was asked by the bishop to coordinate the development of a program for the entire diocese and implement it as a pilot project in her own parish, namely, to receive minor offenders sentenced by the court to do community service as an alternative sentence. The program was well received in her parish and has been implemented in other parishes since then.

Sister Maureen, in addition to the usual pastoral duties, focused her energies on helping the laity adjust to six different parish priests within ten years, some of whom were not prone to consult the community that had been relatively stable for many years. On the national level, she participated with more than two thousand religious in the National Religious Life Congress in Aparecida do Norte, SP. Responding to her love for the environment, Maureen initiated a reflection group via Skype on Ecological Integrity and attended a retreat on spirituality and ecology sponsored by the SSJs of Pembroke in Canada.

Continuing her work on the national secretariat of CPT (Pastoral Land Commission), Sister Jean coordinated the team that digitalized the documentation of land and labor conflicts, eventually making over 400,000 images available on the internet—the largest collection of land conflicts available anywhere in Brazil. She served two terms on the National Coordination of CPT, from 2015 to 2021, during which time she participated in 2017 in the network of people representing Churches and NGOs at a meeting promoted by the World Council of Churches in Maputo, Mozambique to study the impact of corporate financialization on rural communities that live on subsistence agriculture and family farming.[2]

April 2016 was the celebration of the Eleventh National Encounter of the Sisters of St. Joseph in Brazil—totaling 61 participants—organized and hosted by our sisters at a retreat center in Goiânia. And, of course, the seed of the Associates was sprouting. By the end of 2016, a group of men and women in Goiânia were interested in pursuing the values and spirit of the Sisters of St. Joseph, and in April of 2018 sixteen women and men made their commitment as Associates during a liturgy in the church of *Jesus de Nazaré*. In February of 2020, two Associates participated with the sisters in the Seventh Latin American Seminar of Sisters of St. Joseph in Itu, São Paulo.[3]

UBERLÂNDIA

Five hours away, Sisters Ireny and Marlena were equally engaged, responding to new invitations and perceived needs. Sister Ireny, ever-faithful to her position as school secretary, as well as accompanying her parish of *São Benedito*, was active in the Encounters sponsored by the CRB, video conferences with the Latin American SSJs, and traveled to Mexico in 2013 for a live Encounter with the SSJ network, as well as participating in the 2015 General Chapter of the SSJs in Rochester. Sister Marlena continued accompanying Fr. Baltazar in ministering to the rural settlements of migrants outside of Uberlândia which, because of the fluid population, meant reorganizing the sacramental programs every year. In addition, various communities called on her to lead retreat days for their parishes, their youth groups, and their extraordinary ministers. Marlena was also invited to guide a retreat for the diocesan seminarians in July 2016, as well as take on translation duties for the Benedictine monks in Mineiros, Goiás and the SSJs in Norway.

BEYOND THE BIG CITIES

Sister Anne, in the last year of the Felisburgo community (2015) was instrumental with Sister Ellen in obtaining an SSJ Ministry Foundation Grant for the construction of *Creche Ciranda* (a childcare facility) in one of the encampments. Sister Christel Burgmaier, continuing to volunteer as needed in the surgical unit at the Municipal Hospital in Paranaiguara, was the current Regional Coordinator in Brazil and, thus, part of the formal evaluation of the experimental Felisburgo community. To her delight, she discovered the positive value of such an intercongregational community for both the sisters and the church community. In addition to all her pastoral work, Sister Chris was helping with the Children's Pastoral in four communities which included, among other responsibilities, weighing more than two hundred children to record how they are thriving.[4]

As part of her work as a paid secretary/treasurer for the Conference of Religious (CRB), Sister Maureen became aware of another intercongregational community in Bertópolis in the diocese of Teofilo Otoni, Minas Gerais, for which Sister Ellen volunteered. From Ellen's lived perspective, this particular experiment in intercongregational living was not as successful as the Felisburgo endeavor because two of the four sisters were more comfortable praying in the convent than interacting with the people in the outlying regions. After Sister Suzanne Wills passed away in spring 2014, Ellen relocated from Bertopolis to Felisburgo until the completion of that mission in 2015. As Ellen frequently reminded everyone: she was "not taking Sue's place, only her slot. No one could take Sue's place in the hearts of the people."[5]

The next year, with Sister Anne, Ellen joined yet another intercongregational community in Baliza, GO., six hours by car and eight hours by bus from Goiânia. This new group of four was assigned to accompany the people of the *Assentamento Oziel Alves Pereira* (new agricultural settlement named for a murdered activist), a group of 535 small family farms. Because there was no house for the sisters in the *assentamento* for the first years, they stayed in families' homes. Later, when a parish house in town was provided for them by the diocese with a "Support House" (*Casa de Apoio*) in the center of the *assentamento* quite a distance away, the sisters chose to live half the week in town and the other half with families in their assigned five communities in the rural area where they met with them for Bible study, liturgy planning, and preparation for baptisms.[6]

In these years of stretching toward the 'more,' there were also several accolades. Sister Marie José completed her certification in Real Estate law; Sister Marlena assumed the coordination of the CRB nucleus for Uberlândia; Sister Joana received a "Leadership Recognition" award from the Dean of the Pontifical Catholic University of Goiás; and Sister Jean and her work with the Land Pastoral was featured in an article in *Mundo Novo* based on a March 2019 conversation with her in the Global Sisters Report (NCR). That publicity spiraled into an interview with journalist Elizabeth Barber for a feature article in *The New Yorker* magazine.[7]

These new undertakings were not merely jobs or activities of good will. They were not merely "what's next on the horizon that I can get involved in?" The sisters regarded each act of stretching to be present to people as a vocational responsibility grounded in prayer and in the charism of the Sisters of St. Joseph. Since their first days in Brazil, the sisters understood and practiced the SSJ imperative in their early documents of "quartering the city," being present to the "dear neighbor," and "doing all that a woman is capable of doing." The charism, that is, the special gift of the Sisters of St. Joseph for the Church, finds its primary source in each sister's baptismal call, her vocation as a Sister of St. Joseph, and her unique call to minister in Brazil. Rooted in the legacy of the first sisters in Le Puy, France, as well as articulated in our twentieth-century *Constitution*, the Sisters of St. Joseph are committed to serving the "neighbor without distinction."[8] They strive, with all in the family of Joseph, to "unite all people with God and one another . . . by their various ministries of presence, prayer, and service."[9] Their particular way of responding to the Gospel, that is, "the manner of their life, service, and community," reflects the charism of the Sisters of St. Joseph to be a unifying love in the world.[10] "Practical mysticism" is how philosopher-theologian Sister Joan Roccasalvo CSJ defines the SSJ charism. Her description is worth quoting in its entirety. "Theirs is a practical mysticism: union with God found in the ordinary, performed with extraordinary reverence and beauty, with the most profound humility and the most cordial charity toward everyone they encounter."[11] In the words of Sister Carol Zinn, CSJ "You don't have the charism; the charism has you!" Energized by that charism, a Sister of St. Joseph is unafraid to step up and step out to meet the current need—to risk. She makes every effort to "be inclusive, unifying love, and to hold the entire suffering world in her heart."[12] It is this charism that keeps the mission alive and the SSJ community interaction vital. Although 14th century Meister Eckhart precedes the founding of the Sisters of St. Joseph by more than three hundred years, his prayerful vision set in poetic form, captures the contemplative stance and motivating force of our sisters in Brazil:

Oh, teach me in each moment
of every Now to know that
You are the Here in all my
wandering and the Yes in
all my wondering and the Love
in nothing less than everything.[13]

Drum roll. Just when ministry and intentional presence were moving forward, and new ministerial challenges looked promising, the Covid-19 pandemic hit. Liturgical services and most parish meetings were suspended. Zoom became a way of life for countless thousands, and the sisters were hard at work making masks to hand out to people bewildered by the health crisis. The fledging Associates in Goiânia shifted to WhatsApp on their phones to connect with each other, as well as periodic online meetings with the sisters, offering stirring testimony to their commitment to living out the charism, even though their re-commitment ceremony and the reception of the next group had to be postponed for more than a year.

NEGOTIATING THE PANDEMIC

What to do? How to respond to ongoing needs when the Brazilian government was not taking the pandemic seriously? The very rhythm of life had changed. Virtual meetings became the norm and opportunities for more in-service programs were available to the sisters.

At their 2017 Regional Assembly, the sisters had reflected on their presence and ministerial priorities in relation to the needs of that time. Now confronted with a new reality, they revised their priorities for 2020-2023, focusing on sharing their charism and mission[14] and inviting others to walk with them. Specifically, they committed themselves to two objectives: 1) "Join forces with the people in their struggles for social justice and in defense of the Earth, our Common Home; and 2) Cultivate relationships in solidarity, respecting the uniqueness of each person, as an integral part of our charism and mission."

Each objective lent itself to suitable Action Steps such as encouraging collaboration with the Brazilian SSJ Associates and appropriate groups for a common project; promoting social and ecological justice; creating safe spaces for dialogue between families and vulnerable young people, as well as insuring moments of leisure and community life for the sisters themselves. On the practical level, these commitments translated into greater hospitality and use of the house in Goiânia, chatting with parishioners after Mass, joining a group of elderly widows weekly to pray the rosary, distributing the annual SSJ Brazil calendar to those among whom they live and minister, and reinforcing a respect for the land by creating friendly and sacred spaces. Ever creative, each sister found unique ways to be present, serve, and keep connection with the people.

Sister Ellen, for example, limited her craniosacral therapy in Goiânia—with appropriate precautions—to people in a few houses who were willing to follow health protocols. Sister Anne, taking some sabbatical time in the States, returned to Baliza as a driver for the sisters in that rural settlement, and, after completing twenty-five years in Brazil, felt called to return permanently to the States in January 2023. Sister Jean, once frequently on the road to various sites in Brazil for the CPT, adjusted to working from home, assisting the new members of the national coordination, and accompanying and advising the regional teams in the states of Amazonas, Pará and Amapá. Sister Joana was able to establish a few partnerships with like-minded organizations to combat hunger, conduct a vaccine campaign, and return to translation work—but virtually. In her leadership role with the Association of Education, Culture and Citizenship (ADEC), Joana supported the production of geriatric diapers and located companions for patients in palliative care.

Sister Maureen, while still active in formation work, found an internet course on the "Economy of Francesco" and participated in the "Roots Alive" program initiated by Sisters St. Luke Hardy and Beth LeValley of the Rochester SSJs and sponsored by the SSJ Federation. Although home visits in Goiânia were greatly limited, Maureen inaugurated a new group—Parish Pastoral for Integral Ecology—that is gradually evolving. Sister Maria José, within her parish structure which did not shut down completely, was able to coordinate and train thirty-eight new Eucharistic ministers. In Uberlândia, Sister Ireny was working from home and allowed to go to the school building once a week; Sister Marlena was appointed "deaconess" for five rural communities while Fr. Baltazar recovered from surgery, and accompanied Fr. Alan in two more communities. By Christmas time, Marlena was once again able to operate her "cookie factory" making the people's favorite recipes and continuing her "telephone ministry" to make Jesuit Fr. Tabosa's reflections available to 150 people on WhatsApp. In Paranaiguara, Sister Christel reported that most of the people were watching Mass on TV, and she feared they would not return to church when the pandemic subsided—yet for the novena of the Immaculate Conception (December 8), the church was reasonably full. Because her Eucharistic ministers could not enter most houses, they set up an area outside each house for the residents to receive Jesus in Holy Communion. Although officially retired, once again Chris found herself during October 2020 volunteering in the recently renovated hospital operating room with a newly trained staff. Her presence and skill guaranteed that quality medical care could continue on schedule.

ONWARD TO THE 2020S

The Annual Reports of the Brazilian sisters indicates that the three years 2020-2022 were difficult for everyone. In addition to Covid-19 being a significant factor, no new sisters were choosing to join the communities in Brazil, though a few sisters changed ministries. Two sisters continued to serve in Uberlândia, Minas Gerais, seven in the state of Goiás: four in Goiânia, two in Baliza and one in Paranaiguara. Brazilian native Sister Ireny was elected Regional Coordinator in 2020 and began a second term in 2023. As the pandemic became more rampant, vacations were postponed, the January and May SSJ Regional Assemblies in Brazil were held virtually, but, thankfully, in person in September in Goiânia. In April 2021, Sister Jean concluded her six years of service in the National Coordination of the CPT and helped organize the virtual Elective Assembly, due to the uncertainty of air travel restrictions for the delegates. In September 2021, Sister Maureen ended her three-year term as coordinator of the Regional CRB.

Although the pandemic in Brazil worsened during the first months of 2022, some gatherings—with appropriate safeguards—were possible. Sister Maria José, for example, was able to celebrate her twenty-fifth Jubilee, as well as her 50th birthday, with her community in Estrela Dalva and later in her hometown of Cachoeira Alta. The initial group of Associates was finally able to renew their commitments, with six new Associates making their promises for the first time. The Pilgrimage of Martyrs was held in July 2022 with five sisters participating. In October, photovoltaic panels were installed on the house in Recanto do Bosque to continue the sisters' commitment to ecological awareness and innovations. By 2022 some travel was permissible with Sister Jean going to Halifax, Canada to represent the CPT at the Orientation Assembly of "Caritas Canadian." Sister Joana was able to respond in person to a translating opportunity in Pennsylvania, another in Rome, and then meet Sister Marlena in Israel after Marlena's three weeks of translating at the International House of the SSJs in Le Puy. Yet the virtue of stretching toward the 'more' was not limited only to the Sisters of St. Joseph in Brazil. A ripple effect was felt in the States and in Europe through the "Holy Moly Marathon."

This exciting enterprise, initiated by Sister Christel Burgmaier's nephew-in-law, Eyal Feldman raised significant money to support Chris' annual Christmas Food Drive in Paranaiguara. In July 2022, six-foot-plus Eyal completed a ten-mile non-stop Charity Swim around Chicago's Lake Michigan shoreline, raising over $6,200 which provided food for more than 350 Brazilian families. In July 2023, he completed a twelve-mile swim across Lake Constance in Europe. After weather delays and frustrating strong currents, Eyal swam from Germany to Switzerland to Austria and back, completing the challenge in seven hours and forty-five minutes and raising over $9,000 for Sister Chris's project.[15] His connection to the SSJ charism, to the value of risk, and the spiritual power of presence is noteworthy. While not Catholic and not living in Brazil, Eyal Feldman is surely part of the "family of Joseph." Moreover, his commitment to the poor and his admiration of Chris' ministry is contagious. The influence of the Sisters of St. Joseph and their charism continues. What the future holds is still in the mind of God—many seeds planted, waiting to break open and flourish.

2024

THE UPCOMING 60TH anniversary of the Sisters of St. Joseph in Brazil will be a less elaborate celebration than the 50th for obvious reasons. The number of sisters is fewer, and some are uncomfortable about having another big celebration focused on them only 10 years after the big celebrations of the 50th. Four sisters are in their 80s (Jean, Chris, Ellen, Marlena), one in her 70s (Maureen), one in her 60s (Ireny) and two in their 50s (Joana and Maria José). The sisters continue to serve in two states: Minas Gerais and Goiás, with houses in Uberlândia, Goiânia, and Paranaiguara. Of the thirty-seven sisters who have served in Brazil over the past sixty years, Katherine Popowich and Suzanne Wills, both who died in Brazil, are buried in *Jardim do Cerrado* in Goiânia. Nevertheless, the family of Joseph is expanding.

In Rochester, there are 60+ Associates with five more candidates preparing to make their promises. In Brazil there are 20 active Associates in Goiânia, and another smaller group of four in Uberlândia, who recently made their commitment. The "practical mysticism" of contemplation and action continues to animate both sisters and Associates who are committed to stepping out and stepping up to help the "dear neighbor." Energized by that same charism as the Sisters of St. Joseph of Rochester, they assent to the 2023 Chapter Direction Statement to "listen with courage to the urgings of the Spirit and dare to say 'yes.'"[1]

Certainly there are multiple challenges facing all of us in this current world. As the Gospel reminds us, the poor will always be with us. Everywhere the gap between the "haves" and "have nots " is increasing. Similarly, there are large challenges within the Church. Over the last few decades, the collaborative or horizontal model (referred to in Chapter 5) that the early sisters experienced has, in many instances, been replaced by a hierarchical or vertical model in which "Father" makes all the decisions. Such tension between viewpoints raises a perennial question: What is the place of women religious in this Church?

Thankfully, over the long haul, the pendulum of mindsets swings—and, indeed, Pope Francis is accelerating that swing. His commitment to a "field hospital" church and pastors who "smell like sheep" validates his initiative to create a four-year world synod process. In October 2023, more than 360 bishops, priests, lay men and women (with full voting privileges) convened for the first session in Rome to listen, discern, and share their insights on major issues in the contemporary Church. While many people were disappointed that the forty-page summary of the discussions does not mention women deacons or our LGBTQ+ brothers and sisters, the document does offer important perceptions and recommendations about refugees, migrants, human trafficking, and the poor. It recognizes the need to foster peace and protect the Earth, stresses the importance of ecumenism and interreligious cooperation, expresses a desire for better formation of clergy and laity, as well as the "need to make liturgical language more accessible to the faithful and more embodied in the diversity of cultures." And it argues for the Church to be more synodal.[2] Pope Francis himself in his homily at the closing Mass of the first session in Rome, emphasized the value of the *process*, not the outcome: "Today we do not see the full fruit of this process, but with farsightedness we look to the horizon opening up before us."[3]

Surely this report is a sign of hope that the pendulum is swinging toward a more horizontal view of Church. Both Cardinals Blase Cupich of Chicago and Robert McElroy of San Diego indicated that it would be "impossible" to return to an era in which lay men and women are not given both a voice and a vote in major Vatican meetings.[4] As National Catholic Reporter Michael Sean Winters testified, this synod was a milestone in reception of Vatican II: "The rebalancing of Roman Catholic ecclesiology in the past 150 years is now complete. Primacy gave way to collegiality and now to a synodality involving the entire people of God."[5]

The Sisters of St. Joseph in both Rochester and Brazil are facing the same questions as all religious congregations today: How is the future unfolding? What does this mean for aging members? Are we seeing a new flaring out of our charism? Perhaps the most astute question is the oft-repeated refrain from Nancy Schreck OSF: "What if the greatest contribution of religious life has not yet been made?"[6] The Brazilification of our mission in South America indicates that any decisions about the future need to emerge from the sisters there. Our SSJ *Constitution* reinforces this disposition of trust, listening, and waiting for "The Good Rain" to fall on fertile soil: "We trust that the same Spirit who gave being to a congregation of women who dared to undertake all things for the glory of God will continue to call us to serve with courage and fidelity."[7] That same courage and fidelity were formulated in our early 17th century documents and captured by Fr. Marius Nepper S.J. in the translation project of the primitive SSJ documents (1969-72). His poetic "A Portrait of a Daughter of Joseph" is as true today as it was in the 17th century and applies to each member of the "family of Joseph," female and male.

A Portrait of a Daughter of Joseph

Eyes open to the world both miserable and sinful,

> but a world worked on by the Holy Spirit;

Eyes open and ears attentive to the sufferings of the world;

Eyes open, ears attentive and spirit alert.. . .

> never settled down, always in a holy disquietude, searching. . .

> in order to understand,

> to divine what God and the dear neighbor

> await from her today, now, for the body and for the soul;

Eyes open, ears attentive, spirit alert. . .sleeves rolled up for ministry,

> without excluding the more humble, the less pleasing,

> the less noticeable;

Finally, in her face the reflection of a virtue proper to our Congregation,

> – continual joy of spirit..

This is the quiet inner glow of the Sister whose life

> in the service of Jesus Christ has been successful.[8]

This "holy disquietude" must be the guiding disposition of the sisters, Associates, and all the members of the family of Joseph as the story continues and our future unfolds.

End Notes

Chapter 1:
1. Brazil Annual Reports 2001-2004, SSJ Archives.
2. Conversation with Sisters Anne Marvin, Joana Dalva Alves Mendes, Maureen Finn, May 24, 2023.
3. Conversation with Sister Anne Marvin, May 1, 2023.
4. Conversation with Sister Anne Marvin, May 1, 2023.
5. Conversation with Sister Anne Marvin, May 1, 2023.
6. Statistics from Wikipedia.
7. Conversation with Sister Jean Bellini, July 18, 2023.
8. Brazil Annual Report 2004, SSJ Archives.
9. Conversation with Sister Maureen Finn, May 24, 2023.
10. Brazil Annual Report, 2004. SSJ Archives.
11. Brazil Annual Report, 2004. SSJ Archives.
12. Brazil Annual Report 2005, SSJ Archives; Memories of Sisters Anne, Joana, and Maureen, May 24, 2023.
13. Brazil Annual Report, 2004, p. 2. SSJ Archives; additional details provided by Sister Maureen Finn, June 20, 2023.
14. Brazil Annual Report, 2003. SSJ Archives.
15. Conversation with Sister Anne Marvin, May 1, 2023.
16. Brazil Annual Report, 2004, p. 13. SSJ Archives.

Chapter 2:
1. Brazil Annual Reports 2005-2007. SSJ Archives.
2. Conversation with Sister Jean Bellini, July 18, 2023.
3. Brazil Annual Report, 2006, p. 13. SSJ Archives.
4. Conversations with Sister Maureen Finn, June 8 and June 20, 2023.
5. Brazil Annual Report 2005, p.2. SSJ Archives.
6. Brazil Annual Report 2005, p. 18. SSJ Archives.
7. Brazil Annual Report 2006, p. 8. SSJ Archives.
8. Brazil Annual Report 2007, p. 2. SSJ Archives.
9. Conversation with Sister Ellen Kuhl, September 12, 2023.
10. Brazil Annual Report 2006, p. 2. SSJ Archives.
11. Brazil Annual Report 2005, p. 25; Conversation with Sister Marlena Roeger, July 19, 2023.
12. Conversation with Sister Anne Marvin, June 8, 2023.
13. Brazil Annual Report 2008. SSJ Archives; Conversation with Sister Anne Marvin, February 22, and July 19, 2023.
14. Conversation with Sister Maureen Finn, June 20, 2023.

15. Brazil Three-Year Report 2005-2007. SSJ Archives.
16. Brazil Annual Report 2006, p. 7. SSJ Archives.
17. Brazil Annual Report 2006, p. 13. SSJ Archives.

Chapter 3:
1. Brazil Three-Year Report 2008-2010. SSJ Archives.
2. Brazil Annual Report 2009, p. 10. SSJ Archives.
3. Stephen F. Covey, *The Seven Habits of Highly Effective People.* New York: Simon and Schuster, Anniversary Edition 2013.
4. K. Rahner, "The Theology of Risk," *The Furrow*, Vol 19, (May 1968), pp. 266-268. https://www.jstor.org/stable/i27659665.
5. Interview with Martha Mortensen-Kolkmann June 27, 2023.
6. Brazil Annual Report, p. 9. SSJ Archives.
7. www.isjrochester.com.br
8. Brazil Annual Report 2007, p. 12. SSJ Archives.

Chapter 4:
1. Chris Hadfield had a distinguished career as a test pilot and in 1992 became an astronaut. Over the course of his career, he achieved a series of Canadian firsts: he was the first Canadian to be a space mission specialist, to operate the Canadarm in orbit, to do a space-walk and to command the International Space Station.
2. For more information about risk-taking, see https://www.master-class.com/articles/how-to-take-risks#5SlJQsuUZCHk6KM9mex-TMI, downloaded July 18, 2023.
3. Brazil Annual Report 2009, p. 17. SSJ Archives.
4. E-mail from Sister Maureen Finn to Sister Marilyn Pray, January 12, 2009.
5. Brazil Annual Report 2009, p. 17. SSJ Archives.
6. Rahner, p. 268.
7. Excerpts from a letter from Sister Anne Marvin to Sister Marilyn Pray, May 4, 2009.
8. Brazil Annual Report 2009, p. 18. SSJ Archives.
9. Brazil Annual Report 2009, p. 18. SSJ Archives.
10. Conversation with Sister Anne Marvin about her fond memories of Felisburgo, January 28, 2023.
11. Letter from Sister Anne Marvin to Sister Marilyn Pray, May 4, 2009; conversation with Sister Anne, February 22, 2023.

12. Anecdote provided by Sister Anne Marvin, February 22, 2023
13. Brazil Annual Report 2009, p. 18. SSJ Archives.
14. Brazil Annual Report 2009, p. 19. SSJ Archives.
15. Brazil Three-Year Report 2005-2007. SSJ Archives.
16. Letter from "Your sisters in Goiânia" to the SSJ Sisters, Associates, Collaborators. nd (2011).
17. Proposal to Build, June 21, 2011. SSJ Archives.
18. Letter from "Your sisters in Goiânia" to the SSJ Sisters, Associates, Collaborators. nd (2011).
19. SSJ Newsletter July 27, 2012. SSJ Archives.
20. SSJ Newsletter Oct 26, 2012. SSJ Archives.

Chapter 5:
1. Brazil Annual Report 2011, p. 10. SSJ Archives.
2. Brazil Annual Report 2011, p. 1. SSJ Archives.
3. Brazil Annual Report 2011, p. 1. SSJ Archives.
4. Brazil Annual Report 2011, p.10. SSJ Archives.
5. Brazil Annual Report 2011, p. 13. SSJ Archives.
6. Brazil Annual Report 2011, p. 10. SSJ Archives.
7. Brazil Annual Report 2011, p. 17. SSJ Archives.
8. Brazil Annual Report 2011, p. 19. SSJ Archives; conversation with Sister Anne Marvin, February 22, 2023.
9. Conversation with Sister Maureen Finn, June 20, 2023.
10. Anecdote provided by Sister Maureen Finn, June 8, 2023.
11. Anecdote provided by Sister Maureen Finn with additional details from Sister Barbara Staropoli, June 8, 2023.
12. The insight that Brazification had taken placed is from a conversation with Sister Mary Ann Mayer, December 27, 2022.
13. Brazil Annual Report 2011, p. 2. SSJ Archives.
14. Conversation with Sister Jean Bellini, June 18, 2023.
15. Conversation with Sister Anita Kurowski, July 31, 2023.
16. Promulgation of Chapter Direction Statements, Sisters of St. Joseph Chapter, July 2023.

Chapter 6:
1. Ministry report from Sister Katherine in Brazil Annual Report 2005, p. 12. SSJ Archives.
2. Ministry report from Sister Katherine in Brazil Annual Report 2005, p. 12. SSJ Archives.
3. Council that oversees units of SUS (Unified Health System) which

is one of the largest and most complex public health systems in the world, ranging from Primary Care, Urgent Care and hospitals, to organ transplantation, guaranteeing full, universal and free access for the entire population, whether Brazilian citizen or not

4. Brazil Annual Report 2005, p. 13. SSJ Archives.
5. Conversation with Sister Joana Mendes, November 8, 2023.
6. Brazil Annual Report 2007, p. 5. SSJ Archives.
7. Sister Ellen Kuhl supported Sister Katherine's decision to be in a public hospital, despite the inconveniences and wait times.
8. Conversation with Sister Ellen Kuhl, September 12, 2023.
9. Letter from Sister Anne Marvin to the Sisters of St. Joseph of Rochester about Katherine's final days, April 12, 2012.
10. Tribute to Sister Katherine, Bishop Matthew H. Clark, *Catholic Courier*, Diocese of Rochester, April 18, 2012.
11. Email from Sister Maria José to the SSJs in Rochester, April 2012.
12. Author of *Pedagogy of the Oppressed*, Paz e Terra, 1970; 30th Anniversary edition published by Continuum, 2000.
13. *Faith on the Periphery of the World*, by Leonardo Boff, Vozes, 1978.
14. Conversation with Sister Jean Bellini, September 5, 2023.
15. Conversation with Sister Joana, May 24, 2023.
16. The Myky indigenous tribe maintained isolation from the surrounding non-indigenous population until 1971; hence in the 1990s the tribe was not that removed from their traditional way of living.
17. Email from Sister Anne Marvin to the Sisters of St. Joseph of Rochester detailing events leading up to Suzanne's illness and death, June 26, 2014.
18. Conversation with Sister Anne Marvin recounting her memories of Sue's last weeks and funeral, February 22,2023.
19. Conversation with Sister Jean Bellini, September 5, 2023.
20. Email from Sister Anne Marvin to the Sisters of St. Joseph of Rochester detailing events leading up to Suzanne'sillness and death, June 26, 2014.
21. Conversation with Sister Ellen Kuhl, September 12, 2023.
22. This community was started by Sisters Suzanne Wills and Ellen Kuhl in the 1990s.
23. Both Sisters Jean and Anne overheard various people insist that that Sue would retire in their town or community; conversation with Sister Anne Marvin, February 22, 2023.
24. Comments shared by Sister Maureen Finn in an email to Sister

Monica Weis, November 5, 2023.
25. Conversation with Sister Maureen Finn, October 3, 2023.
26. SSJ Newsletter, May 11, 2018 and May 10, 2019.
27. Sister Maureen Finn in the SSJ Newsletter May 10, 2019.

Chapter 7:
1. Brazil Annual Report 2013, p. 6. SSJ Archives.
2. Brazil Annual Report 2013, p. 10. SSJ Archives.
3. Details of the celebration were recounted by Sisters Ellen Kuhl, Jean Bellini, Marlena, Anne Marvin, Christel Burgmaier, in a gathering on August 14, 2023.
4. After more than 40 years in Brazil, Sister Barbara Orczyk returned to the United States in 2010 to care for her ailing mother; served on congregational Leadership from 2011-2015; then volunteered at St. Stanislaus parish until her own health failed. She later died at the Sisters of St. Joseph Motherhouse on May 4, 2023.
5. Historical data on Paranaiguara provided by Sister Christel Burgmaier, August 18, 20223.
6. Brazil Annual Report 2014 plus memories of Sisters Ellen, Marlena, Jean, Marlena, Anne, and Christel.

Chapter 8:
1. Lula da Silva's case was later annulled, and the judge and prosecutor of his case were accused of collusion.
2. da Silva was released in November 2019.
3. Brazil Annual Report 2017. SSJ Archives.
4. Conversation with Sister Maureen Finn, October 20, 2023.
5. Brazil Annual Report 2015. SSJ Archives.
6. Conversation with Sister Ellen Kuhl, September 12, 2023.
7. Brazil Annual Report 2015. SSJ Archives.
8. Elizabeth Barber, "A Nun's Journey in the Amazon" in *The New Yorker*, February 17, 2020.
9. "Identity," para #5, *Constitution/Complementary Document*, Sisters of St. Joseph of Rochester, New York, 1987.
10. "Ministry," para #24, *Constitution/Complementary Document*, Sisters of St. Joseph of Rochester, New York, 1987.
11. "Identity," para #3, *Constitution/Complementary Document*, Sisters of St. Joseph of Rochester, New York, 1987.
12. Joan L. Roccasalvo, CSJ. *The Ignatian Influence of the Spirit of the Sisters of St. Joseph*. Montrose Publishing Company, 1993.

13. Sister Carol Zinn, CSJ, Executive Director of the Leadership Conference of Women Religious (YouTube, March 15, 2015).

14. *Meister Eckhart's Book of the Heart: Meditations for the Restless Soul*, edited by Jon M. Sweeney and Mark S. Burrows. Hampton Roads Publishing, 2017, p. 21.

15. Brazil Three-Year Report 2020-2023. SSJ Archives.

16. SSJ Newsletter, September 10, 2023. Eyal and his family were welcomed at the SSJ Motherhouse in Rochester in August 2023. He has plans for a 2024 Holy Moly Marathon Swim.

Epilogue:

1. Promulgation of Chapter Direction Statements, Sisters of St. Joseph of Rochester, July 2024.

2. Thomas Reese, "Synod on synodality report is disappointing but not surprising," *National Catholic Reporter*, November 3, 2023. [https://www.ncronline.org>opinion.guest-voices]

3. Carol Glatz, "Pope Francis closes synod with 'dream' of a church with open doors," *National Catholic Reporter*, October 29, 2023. [https://www.ncronline.org>vatican>vatican-news/pope-francis]

4. Joshua J. McElwee, "Exclusive: Cardinals Cupich, McElroy say 'impossible to go back' to synods without lay voters," *National Catholic Reporter*, October 30, 2023. [https://www.ncronline.org/vatican/ vatican-news/exclusive].

5. Michael Sean Winters, "Synod is a Milestone in the Reception of Vatican II." [https://www.realclearreligion.org>2023/10/30>synod].

6. unsigned interview with Sister Teresa Maya, CCVI, President of LCWR, "What Religious orders Can Do Today to Thrive" *US Catholic* Vol 83: 3 pp. 34-37 (March 19, 2018). [https:/uscatholic.org>March 2018].

7. "Identity,"para #6, *Constitution/Complementary Document*, Sisters of St. Joseph of Rochester, New York, 1987.

8. Marius Nepper, SJ: This portrait is based on the extensive research done by Fr. Nepper on the founding documents of the congregation. [https://cssjfed.org/resources/spirituality/]

About the Author

Monica Weis, SSJ, Professor of English Emerita at Nazareth University, has been a Fulbright Visiting Professor at the University of Pannonia in Veszprém, Hungary, active for more than twenty years in the International Thomas Merton Society, and the author of *Thomas Merton's Gethsemani: Landscapes of Paradise* (UPK 2005), *The Environmental Vision of Thomas Merton* (UPK 2011), and *Thomas Merton and the Celts* (Wipf and Stock 2016).

Made in the USA
Columbia, SC
31 August 2024

40800953R00070